CONTENTS

PAGE
FOREWORD 1
PREFACE 2
BROADMOOR OCTOBER 2001 3
AGED 20: BROADMOOR 3
AGED 6: THE NEIGHBOURHOOD 9
AGED 7: THE GUN POSSE 13
AGED 8: WEED 17
AGED 11: YOUNG BLOODS 19
AGED 12: POLICE AND THIEVES 24
AGED 13: CRACK AND GUNS 30
AGED 14: GUNMAN POINT 33
AGED 15: KIDULTHOOD 37
AGED 16: CREEPING 40
AGED 16 (cont'd): BUSINESS MAN 43
AGED 17: ROCKS AND DANCES 47
AGED 18: NEW JACK KIDS 53
AGED 18: CRACK KING 62
AGED 18 (cont'd): TIME OUT 64
AGED 18 (cont'd): SNOOP 67
AGED 19: MADNESS 72
AGED 19 (cont'd): BUCKY 76
AGED 19 (contd): VOICES 80

(5 months before the killings)
AGED 19 (cont'd): JUDGEMENT DAY 84
AGED 19 (cont'd): WAR 88
AGED 20: THE AFTERMATH 91
AGED 33: ENDINGS

REDEMPTION

FOREWORD

The first time I heard Wayne Hutchinson tell his story was on some tapes recorded in Broadmoor high-security psychiatric hospital. He'd sent them to me because he'd read my book "Street Boys: 7

Kids. 1 Estate. No way out about the lives of a young street gang in Brixton. He'd been one of the older boys who'd taught the younger ones the rules of South London street life: how to sell drugs, where to get guns, who to respect, when to keep quiet. Most of the boys came through that life intact. Some of them turned their lives around. But Wayne Hutchinson didn't survive gang life. Something went badly wrong.

He was born at a turning point in British society: the moment when street gangs and gun crime first exploded on Britain's streets. From an innocent boy growing up on a London estate he turned to a life of drugs and gangs becoming a major player in a crime wave that still claims the lives of young Britons. Then, at the height of his notoriety as a drug kingpin and gang leader, something cracked. Just after his 19 birthday he went on a six day killing rampage on the streets of London which left two people dead and five seriously injured.

Some of what follows is nasty and shocking. But stick with it. Wayne Hutchinson is a man trying to come to terms with the life he has led and the crimes he's committed. He is still in a secure mental health institution but in the near future he will be out living amongst the rest of us. Reading his story might help us to understand him and learn something about the society we live in. What sort of person commits such evil acts? What makes a man go mad? Can there be redemption and forgiveness? Can acts like this be prevented?

This is Wayne Hutchinson's story told in his voice I have compiled it from therapy tapes and conversations with Wayne during visits to the Royal Bethlem Hospital. Additional material comes from my own research and conversations with his psychiatrists, friends, family and the families of his victims.

PREFACE

Not many people have written a book like this. They are either dead or still on the streets and too frightened because they think the police are going to lock them up. Or they are going to get done in. Many of these books aren't from the actual person's mouth. This one tells the truth from the streets.

I want to show the struggle that young men face on the street. Having wants and needs that ain't satisfied. To show the struggle I faced in my life as a person and also for other young people to see the traps, how easy it is to be led into this way of life.

There's a rap line I wrote that means a lot for me: *God's in us, but the Devil runs the streets. So watch out before he swipes you off your feet.*

The life I've led was stressful, dangerous, betrayal, loss, fear and bang I exploded. I killed people when I wasn't right in my head. I pray to my victims every night. "I'm sorry for taking your lives. I'm sorry for what I done for your families and hoping that you rest in a better place and you are looking down on your families and blessing them." That's what I pray.

With this book I'm trying to pick up all the pieces and like on a rocket, travel back through time to see it all again, to explain it, to see if I can find some answers. To find out what went wrong and when it went wrong. Obviously one day that rocket is going to get to a height and I will see my life more clearly.

I want to try and reach people even though people have condemned me. After all the madness, the mayhem and confusion, I've still got my faculties. I've still got something to say. Maybe it's of use.

Wayne Hutchinson.

Royal Bethlem Psychiatric Hospital, 2009

ROADMOOR October 2001

(7 years after the killings) You wanna get in my shoes? My shoes are worn out, man, I'm tired from my life. How people can be so fucked up? They treat me like I'm some dangerous animal and then they talk to me normal I don't understand that. I'm just trying to keep myself normal. To keep my faith in God. Coz God knows my soul is tired. Seven years ago that happened. Seven years and I've been going through hell. I've been trying to make sense of it for seven years. And they keep on telling me that I'm the key to it. I get the fear. The fear of never being released. The fear of what I've done and how it's playing in my life. And the big fear. Is my soul going to hell? One day your kingdom has to fall. That's life. My kingdom has fallen.

AGED 20: BROADMOOR

Out of all the crazy times in my life, the craziest was my first month in Broadmoor. They took me there in handcuffs from Belmarsh prison, on prison transfer, what they call section 48 49. I didn't want to go. I wanted to stay in prison, not go to a hospital. But my mum said I needed help. "If you go back to prison I won't come and visit you again. You must stay in hospital." Rather than lose contact with my mum I thought it was best to stay there. They put me in Henley unit, in Ronnie Kray's old cell. He'd died a few weeks earlier. That's when I met the other inmates.

There was a notorious killer there, a man who seemed to have an aura of death about him. It was like he was surrounded by cold air I recognized him from the papers. A trimmed beard, slim with cold, dark eyes. The moment I saw him I didn't like him. It was Peter Sutcliffe 'The Yorkshire Ripper'. There was also Kenny Erskine, better known as the Stockwell Strangler. Of course I knew about him.

When I was a kid growing up in Stockwell mothers used to get their kids in early at night coz of this killer stalking the streets. And there I was, a decade later in the same unit as him. The first few days in Broadmoor I got acquainted with the lads on the ward. I learnt quickly that the inmates were running it. At 9pm we would cook in the kitchen, making burgers, watching MTV and smoking dope and drinking vodka. Some of the inmates used to give the staff money to smuggle it in. That's how it worked in Broadmoor. The inmates ran the place. Most of the staff stayed sitting in their own room not paying us any attention. They wouldn't come into the main part of the ward. They let us be coz it was less trouble for them that way. Except there was this one nurse called John who tried to rule the ward with an iron fist. He tried to ruin the parties with his rules but most of the time it was just him against us so we always won out. He kept coming in, trying to confiscate the alcohol. What he didn't know was that one night there was a plan hatched to do away with Sutcliffe. It was this inmate who wanted some notoriety. That was the main object of him getting on that ward. He wanted to do something to someone famous and get famous himself. He wanted to be the man who killed The Ripper. He thought Sutcliffe deserved to die and that people would thank him for it. That's what he kept telling us. Trouble had been brewing for days. We knew it was going to happen. We stayed in the kitchen while this inmate set off towards Sutcliffe's room. We heard the footsteps, we heard the voices, we heard the door opening and closing. We all knew what was going to happen. The inmate had told us how he was going to kill Sutcliffe. He grabbed a cable from the cassette player, wrapped it round Sutcliffe's neck and started pulling. Sutcliffe's head began to flop to one side. It was going to the plan that the inmate had laid out until Kenny Erskine walked past, heard the noises pushed open the door and discovered Sutcliffe being strangled. It was Kenny who pressed the panic button. The Stockwell Strangler saved the Yorkshire Ripper. That's when the staff ran in and pulled the inmate off and released him. It was just in time coz Sutcliffe's head was nodding as though he was on his way out. He was almost on death's doors. That was during my first few weeks in Broadmoor. It was a big load for a 20 year old kid from south west

London who was still trying to come to terms with all that had happened. And there I was locked up in a psychiatric hospital with some of Britain's most notorious prisoners. It was hard getting my head round it. How did I
get here!

BROADMOOR 2000

This is how the Devil works. Imagine the scenario. You're sitting down with a pile of drugs in front of you. You've already smoked a lot and you are thinking you shouldn't have any more and not get in a car coz you will crash it. But the Devil appears and he's going, 'no, you'll be okay. Smoke it." And you smoke it and if was that little bit of power that the Devil has given you. Then the Devil goes, "you might get robbed tonight, go and get your gun out of the drawer and put your gun in your waist." So, you've got that power now and you get in the car with your gun and you get caught by the police. Does the Devil love you or not? You think so, but it's a tricky situation.

I've been there. Know how it works. It's like a little seed and you have to tight that little seed and if you can fight that then you can win but otherwise it 6 can grow and manipulate you. You have to be on your guard man. The Devil is like your best friend sometimes. That's what I was wrestling with all the time. That's how the Devil treats you. He says things to you, "Hang out with me. You can get rid of your money worries and have a good time." The bad man sent me out on a path of destruction and the angel brought me back in here for safety. I want to sort my head out. I ask myself, where is God and what am I meant to learn?

ED 6: THE NEIGHBOURHOOD

I wanted to be a policeman from a young age. There were these TV shows like Chips with the motorbikes and Dukes of Hazard and Starsky and Hutch. Driving cars, guns, it was like action and appealing. But there were no police on my estate, only gangsters. And then I saw that film, I can't remember the name, where the gangster is surrounded by police but he runs up to the roof and there's a helicopter on the roof and that's how he gets away It got to me and I said to myself, even at a young age. "That is the kind of person I want to be.' From then I wanted to be a gangster with a helicopter on the roof, mixing with politicians and the in-crowd. Robert De Niro, Al Pacino, Joe Pesci. Like the Godfather, Scarface, the Untouchables. Gangster stuff. Dress nice. Get money like that. That's what I wanted. I didn't want to be no policeman. I didn't want to join no army. I had three cousins in the army. I wanted to build my own army.

The estate I grew up on was the infamous Stockwell Park estate in south west London, home of bailers, players and Gs, street slang for Gangsters, crooks, hoodlums and drug dealers. It was a concrete estate made up of council blocks connected by bridges. Some were high rise blocks, others were low rise. There were lots of alleyways and paths that connected different parts of the estate. If you didn't live there it was a maze To us though it was like a playground. Stockwell Park estate was the center of my world. It was where I first played, it was where I made my friends, It was where I did most of my crime. It were my freedom, my castle and my kingdom. Me and my two brothers and sister lived with my mum in one of the white concrete blocks called Taylor House at the center of the estate next to the shopping center. My oldest brother Tony was twenty years older than me. Cleo, my sister was twelve years older, Desmond was five years older.

My mum was born in Jamaica and came over to England when she was a teenager. The father of my brothers and sister was killed in a car accident

before I was born. I never knew who my dad was. My mum never told me who my dad was. It became a constant source of worry for me, always in the back of my mind. I was looking out for my dad the whole time. We used to go to church in a Volvo with this brown skinned mart with an afro and all of a sudden he disappeared and I asked my uncle coz I wanted to know. 'Is that my dad?" "Yes, that's your dad." But then I asked my mum and she told me it wasn't him. I was just going round in circles. My brothers and sister, one of them knew but they wouldn't tell me anything. It was one of those mysteries that used to be important to me. Who is my father?
But nobody has ever told me. My name was Wayne but everyone called me Matty. My first strong memory was when I bit the hand of my teacher. It was my first school day and my mum had dropped me off there and I didn't want to go. I didn't want to be away from my mum. My teacher tried to drag me in the classroom with me kicking and pulling away and crying and she continued to pull me into class. At that time I thought the teacher was ignorant for doing that. So I bit her. I remember looking in amazement and seeing blood

drip from her hand. I remember this day very clear because it was the first time I was apart from my mother or family into the care of others.

The only way I would go back to school was wearing red Dunlop Wellington boots. My mum took me to Brixton market and because I was very much into Paddington Bear she bought me a pair just like his. I thought that I wanted to be like him because he always got into trouble and had adventures. My mother wanted to reassure me. "Every time I am away from you, you can wear these boots so that you know that I am there." From then on it was easier. I felt that my mum was with me anytime I had my red boots on. I felt special, very special indeed Trust me. From that first school day I knew I had some anger in me When the older kids stole my Space Invader riding bike I would burst into a rage. The bikes cost 10p to rent for half an hour so it was a big thing when they stole it but I didn't whine and go and get my older brother to sort them out. I just chased the older kids round while they were riding my bike. I was mad with anger. The older kids would just laugh at me and slap me as I chased them but that just made me even more madder. To this day if I hear people laughing it brings an uncomfortable feeling for me, especially if I'm not involved. Even back then as a little kid I had murderous thoughts when the older boys would wind me up, But everyone gets them sometimes don't they I was always hungry. My mum would take me to Brixton Market and meet her friends and be talking for half an hour at a time. I'd be pulling on my mum's coat wanting to get on. 'Come on, mum, we got to go shopping." I'd walk past the chicken shop. "Can I get a junior lunch?" She'd pull me away from the shop. "There's food in the house." I was always hungry and those experiences, being told I couldn't have food, always made me want things that were out my means, always a hunger for more. I guess from an early day there wasn't much time for play. Coz we were always short of money, laughter and fun went out the window and the game was to survive which is a hard thing to do when money breeds greed. I was a listener, not a doer to start. I spent my time listening to the older heads who my brother brought round. They'd be talking about robbing and shotting and thieving and I'd drink up everything they said and work out what role they all played The older heads were

Martin. Dandy, the Mills brothers, the Dimes brothers, Mad Up, the Brothers Grimm, P Jedel and the Yankee Twins. Because I was a fatherless child I took as much information from them as possible. They were the father figures for me.

At weekends and in the evenings I'd join the older heads in the garages underneath the flats on the estate. They'd set up like a camp with wooden boxes and milk bottle crates to sit on. They'd taped sponges to the top to make them more comfortable. That's where they'd smoke and talk I sat with them from a young age sipping Guinness and learning about life. It was good to be around them because I felt they were teaching me. But it can become confusing because on my estate there was this thing about who is the biggest and strongest. I like to be around sensibility. I can't take no foolishness. So I drunk up what the older men told me. This is what I learnt. It's a cruel world. Dog eat dog. Only The strong survive in the environment I was growing up in you had to have a sense of power. That's what the message to me was. You had to be ruthless. They used to take me aside and give me words of advice. "If you want to be a gangster, Star, you gotta shoot them down, bust them up, if they are messin' ya No one said to me, "If you want to be a gangster, then okay. But my advice is be a solicitor." No one ever talked to me on that level. No, they told me about being a gangster, about guns and drugs and how hard it was to make money and how you had to watch your back and beware of the police. No one on my estate wanted the police around coz of the criminal activities.

One summer evening one of the older heads called the police to say that there was a robbery on the estate. They'd carried this washing machine onto one of the bridges that connected the blocks. When the police car came into the estate they pushed the washing machine off the bridge. The thing landed onto the roof of the police car, flattening it and making the officers run for their lives. I remember that evening very clearly. The estate was a criminal's dream. Some of the older guys hit security vans and take refuge on the estate, so less police the better. No one like the police. I was on my way to a wedding in Brixton with my mum.

We were walking up Brixton Road and a woman comes up to us. "If I was you I would turn back now coz there's rioting up there." Suddenly me and my mum found ourselves in the crossfire. Bricks were frying over our heads. The older boys on the estate were breaking windows and turning over cars and being chased by police. There were sirens and fire engines hundreds of police charging into Brixton. We eventually got to a cab station and watched it all on TV at my aunt's house in Peckham. When we got back it seemed like Brixton was burnt to the ground. Cars were overturned, shops were black, the streets were littered with stones, bricks, overturned rubbish bins. It had a big impact on me that did. I was a fatherless child. The older heads who rioted were becoming my heroes. I looked up to the older criminals on the street. They were my father figures. At home we was poor and my mum was struggling. 1 wasn't aware of there being no choice from a young age. I just followed what the older heads on the estate did. And when I followed what the older heads did that led to my first criminal activities. And it was a road that I found more and more difficult to get off.

BROADMOOR, 2000

You're just provoking me, making me talk about these things. There are a lot of things that ain't right and I don t want to know. I don't want to know. I'm trying to live my life. I want to tell my story and move on and get the fuck out of here. I don't want to talk about no past daddy or how it was as a child with no money. I don't want to talk about no pain. The pain ain't going nowhere. The pain is what keeps me alive. If there was no pain I'd be dead. The pain give me the tight to move on. You think I can get rid of pain from just talking. Years of pain. I need some action, I need to kick some ass. I need to see someone suffer like I've suffered. The perpetrators, You can't help me heal. My wounds are too deep. Give up. My lips are burning me. What's going on? I'm falling apart in this place. Leprosy and skin disease have got hold of me. I'm troubled inside for what man has done to me. I'm powerless in this fucking place. Before I was very powerful. I was brought up to be a warrior I feel betrayed and betrayal is the worse thing that can happen. I want to be humble. Don't push my mind. Respect my mind. I want people to know what I went through. When it's finished that's when be satisfied. That's when some of the pain will be gone.

AGED 7: THE GUN POSSE

I went to school but didn't pay much attention. The best part of the day was walking to school and I notice the sun was always in a position following me around until I got to school. And I got home from school and I said to my mum you know the sun always follows me?" "No son, The sun is in the sky. It appears like it's following you because its always there and will always be with you, but it's not following you." I remember that still today. I didn't gel much satisfaction from school. All my excitement was on the estate and I lived for the evenings and weekends. The Greggs were this infamous family on the estate. I was under strict orders not to mix with them but it didn't stop me. I came across them when I ran into one of them at the supermarket. I was there to buy some rice and when the shopkeeper gave me my change, one of them took my change off the counter and ran away with it. My mum marched round to the shopkeeper demanding to know what had happened. She was given her money back but from that moment she told me never to play with them. I didn't listen. By this time f was already playing out with the Gregg's nephews, Sadda and Dracula. Sadda coz he always had a sad expression and Dracula coz he had a v shaped fringe like Christopher Lee in those vampire films. We'd became friends after a fight. I'd beaten up Dracula over something and his older brother Sadda had joined in and beaten me up. From that time we became firm friends. And with Dracula and Sadda we became a new gang of upstarts ready to take on the world. By then we'd moved into a larger four bedroom house on the other side of the estate closest to Brixton.

My brothers and sister were all still living at home at this time and I was sleeping in the front room next to the window in order to let my brother and sister come in coz they went out raving and didn't want my mum to know, But I didn't rely on them coz they were much older than me. Instead I teamed up with the Brothers Grimm. Jinn and Tree and the Crisp brothers, Ton and Pee. We had a gang and swore a blood oath. Our fun was different from other people. We grew up hard and fast. That's what it was like on the estate. Stand or fall. Of course we played football, cards and forty forty, I did all that But even a game like forty forty was not always about having fun. During the game you had to close your eyes and count to forty and find the rest of the crew who would be hiding in garages, and doorways or landings. But it was all to be useful later with our robbing activities. Getting us to know the layout of the estate and where we could hide and where we could run to. The estate was like a big playground for us and cut us off from rest of the world and offered us protection.

The robbing activities started small, stealing sweets, and cans of drinks from local shops. But we were all little kids, hungry for money and toys coz we never got much at home. So, at the weekends we'd all hit the West End. Our first target was Hamleys for toys and it would be hit hard by us. We would rob other children. Most of the time we would send Ton Crisp up first to steal from little kids He was only 4 years old. "Hand over your goods." Some would be so amazed that they'd hand over their toys. The ones who resist we would all surround with bottles and knives.

"Give us your He Man. Give us your Subbuteo. Give us your Star Wars toy." There was not much resistance coz there were so many of us. And we had two older boys with us, Jiveman and Sadda who were both ten years old. Jiveman was Sadda's uncle. Twenty or so of us hollering and rushing at people, hellbent on mayhem and destruction. It's a terrifying sight. I learnt from an early age that terror is a valuable weapon. Soon others joined the gang like Couch, Pony and Dar Stop, Gypsy Martin who lived in a block of flats opposite me and Jimbo lived in the flats behind. Kyle was the leader of the gang and I was second in command. We soon got bored with the Subbuteos and Star Wars and moved onto guns. I'd always been intrigued by guns. Even plastic guns. We'd steal big heavy cap guns from Hamleys and when they were let off they sounded like the real thing. That's when we started calling ourselves the Gun Posse s\ the massive walking around the estate like we were in a Western or Italian gangster movie. Even then we knew that one day we would be running around with real guns Our main game was called the Reject Book. It was like a court case. One of the older guys who had been in the court system,

Papa T. taught us how to play He was a big guy. You had a judge and prosecution and Jurors and each one of us would have to defend himself in front of the others over some crime or stupidity that we'd done, like getting caught by the ticket inspector or breaking something that we'd stolen. "Your honour II weren't me that got caught by the shop keeper. The only witness you have is a well-known liar that appeared before you only yesterday on a charge of ignorance." It was just like a court in a real life setting and them same experiences helped me beat a court case for GBH later on. Who ever got found guilty in the things which were brought up would leave to plan the next movement which might mean robbing, stealing, playing football or even fighting another gang to prove that you were loyal to the gang. The movement had to be carried out without question. One of the most movements we carried out was nicking BMXs coz they were in fashion. We knew we would be able to lose anyone chasing us. We'd pedal into the estate and be gone. Then we would take them to George who would break them up and hand out spare parts which we could put on our own bikes. George's father hated us. If he spied us he'd come down ranting. "You thieving bastards. One day the law going to lock you up. Move from me house before I duck ye with piss water" 10 He pissed into a potty at night and he was always trying to empty it over us. We'd use the BMXs to play "guide and protection," riding up to each other and cutting your opponent up to try and make them fall off the bike. We rode all over the place from north to west London and coz we never had any money on us and we were always hungry we would park outside a 7/11 with our pedals up on the kerb ready to go. I would always attack the Bounty Rack, some would go for the burgers and others would go for the drinks. There might be twenty of us robbing the joint at one time. When it was time to split we'd run out and jump on our bikes. One time I missed my pedals and landed an my nuts but no time to be waiting coz you've just run out of a shop without paying. If one of us got caught we'd go back in there to save him and there would be a big beat down. Can you imagine twenty youths fighting four shopkeepers? It was chaotic.

Then we would ride around the skateboard park in the estate which locals nicknamed Jurassic park because they thought that all the little kids were out of control animals. It was in them days that I also learned about friendship and betrayal. We were a gang that would look out each other but sometimes there were no loyalty. There was a game called penny up where you tossed several coins whoever guessed heads or tails correctly kept all the coins. But Couch lifted my money from the floor even though he hadn't won it. "Give me back my money .° But he wouldn't. It was a tear-up. I was having none of it. I jumped up from the stairs I was sitting on and punched him to the ground, and knocked him down, despite his being twice the size of me I was gonna stomp on his head.   others had to intervene and drag me away. Then Couch came round and swung at me and gave me a black eye. I was fuming. He had dissed me and my rep as fighter in the gang. I never got to hear the last of it. My mum didn't know what we were about for a long time. She was busy earning money, working 9 to 5 for Lambeth Council as an admen assistant in the poll tax sectioned so she couldn't control me too much. But one time me and Sadda and Dracula got arrested for trying to break into the post office.

The police took me back home and told my mum what I'd done. She hit me with everything in the room so bad that my sister had to run to the police. °My mum has gone berserk she is killing him. She is beating him to death." The police had to come back and reassure her that they were not going to prosecute me. It was only then that she stopped beating me. When the police handed over the caution for my mum she read it and lore it up in front of me. "You be careful son. When the police's hand touches you, you will always be in their hands. It will curse the essence of your soul.

BROADMOOR, 2000

The cards are in their hands. I don't know what is going to happen. I don't want nothing to trigger angry thoughts and justice and all I was trying to do what I did outside I don't want to talk about my feelings it just winds me up. It doesn't work for me it just gets me angry. It don't make no sense does it. I don't want to touch on delicate situations. You tell 'em what happens when I'm like that. Tell them to leave me alone when I'm like that. I'm in a peaceful place at the moment. I don't want to talk about pain and frustration, it just makes me mad. Let's go there when I'm drinking champagne when I'm in a club. This place is crazy. Arguments start over sitting in a chair. It's bull shit. It's all so small minded. I can't keep my eyes open. They are burning me. I can feel the pain coming up in my chest. I'm going to explode. Leave me alone.

AGED 8: WEED

The first time I smoked weed was when my friend Kus from school stole some home grown from his dad's garden. We went to my mum's house, put it under the grill until it was all dried up, put it in a brown paper bag and cycled to the playground opposite Brixton
College. That's where we smoked it. It became a regular occurrence. We even started taking it into school until the teachers found us smoking it in the toilet and we got the beating of our lives. It started off just as a little buzz. It's what everyone did on the estate. It was normal. It got even easier when a drug dealer called Muscles moved around the corner to me and I soon became best friends with his youngest son Tank, He was like my little brother.
We would smoke weed and go on drug runs for his father, a kilo of ash strapped to our chest as we headed off on our BMXs. Sometimes his dad would

pay us in cash sometimes in weed. Coz my mum never had any money to give me so the cash was very useful to me. I also got a bit of money from being a lookout for the older heads. I been watching for the others warning them when they were Join' a burglary. When they were doing a burglary on the estate or near the estate I had to tell them if the police were coining. They'd give me a five pound note for my part. I'd take my fiver to Muscles and if I couldn't get any weed off Muscles I'd just steal ash out of my brother's hand when he was asleep.

Another was using a coat hanger and tissue and stuff it down the photo machine at Brixton and Vauxhall tube stations. They were fat meaning they had lots of money in them. The coat hanger would pull up a lever and the tissue would keep it open and the money would come out the rejection compartment and duss out. No one stopped me doing what I wanted to do. My mum was out trying to earn money to keep the family going so I just did as I pleased from a certain age. There was one step-dad figure we used to call "Dada" and "Mr Senior". He took me out but he was drinking too much and the things he used to try and do to my mum used to make me angry. He used to try and hit my mum but she wouldn't have it and would just whack him up. He wasn't a bad man. He was just on too much booze .Whenever I asked about my dad no one would tell me. It's weird. They came up with excuses. I asked family members. "Who is my dad?" 'We're not too sure who he is." Every time I got into trouble I did think about it. I wonder what my father would say? Because I never had a father then I ended up facing the world all by myself.

No one told me the dangers I face from mankind. I was looking for older reasoning so I resort to the local king pin on the street and gel in with their business and I just sit in the corner and smoke a spliff of weed and listen to them speak and you are like, you siphon he good, the bad, the truth and the nonsense out of what they are saying and you build an own picture in your own mind and they become like father figures. And you look up to them. They seemed to have everything a man could want. It wasn't just me. Other kids on the estate were going through the same thing. And that's how it goes. It's a vicious circle and the ones who were children become fathers themselves and they get incarcerated away from their children and so it repeats. There's some serious shit there man. As an aside it was at this time that everyone in Stockwell was panicking about a serial killer — a man who was going round breaking into old women's houses and raping and killing them. The Stockwell Strangler they called him. How was it to know that years later I'd be locked up with him in Broadmoor?

BROADMOOR. 2000

The sun's out been looking at the sun coming in and out all day, wondering what is driving if. Its coming out after all these rains and floods of past few days. So somethings going on. I just need to work it out. Something sometimes tells me that

I'm the cause of these floods. Sometimes it tells me I'm the cause of the sunshine. I've lots of friends who were in this life with me and they are dead.

Sometimes I'm here and I'm thinking about a certain person and a ray of sunshine came out as if to say "I'm looking down on you." Not as good as they used to be back in the day. Ever since I been locked up it don't seem so good. When I played when I was a child the sun was so hot your shoe would be sinking in the tar. And you'd be parching and pouring water over yourself just to cool down. It was lovely man. Nice and cold. Cold. Them were happy days. When I was a child now I'm a man and I got responsibility it's a wicked world but I'm not wicked, I've got a heart. People like to play with it. They think it's a toy.

AGED 11: YOUNG BLOODS

I went to Archbishop Michael Ramsey secondary school in Camberwell. There I met boys from all over South London. From Peckham and Kennington and Lewisham. My horizons expanded. I started making contacts. Later them same contacts would help me, and betray me. They were just mates I hung out with and smoked spliffs with.

When I'd get to school, I'd talk to this guy at school called Vin Parks from Peckham. He was a tall skinny guy with a big nose which is why I called him Gonzo. "Gonzo, got any ash today?" "Yeah. Take this. Pay me tomorrow."

There was usually weed to be had at school. I'd have a puff in the toilets during the breaks. I'd smoke when school was over. If there was any left over by the morning I'd smoke on me way to school.

It became a habit. I started spending money on buying ash, five pounds here and there, then ten pounds, I'd wake up and the first ting I wanted to do was take a spliff. And I'd need it to get through the school day.

We had a teacher we called Ninja and he used to sneak up in the toilets on us and he wouldn't leave us alone. He'd always try and catch us out. I'd have to be careful and stay out of trouble because I knew that if my mum caught me doing bad at school I'd get a beating so I used to have to blag my way out of it. "No teacher. I never smoked nuffin'. I done nuffin'. I don't know who was smoking but it weren't me." And I had to keep that stern look on my face of honesty.

But after a draw I'd be buzzing. It felt good. It felt nice. It was like a new world to me. Weed would give me the instinct to burn, not learn. Books went out the window I'd smoke then half an hour later I'd be all mellow and calm. An hour later I'd be in the classroom and the teacher would be looking at me and I'd be falling asleep. There was this one black teacher, Mrs Evans who taught English and just as I was dropping off she goes to me all furious, "I pay bills and taxes for people like you.

You ain't going to amount to nothing and I'll end up paying your dole money. You are worth nothing."

I went home and told me mum and me mum went mad and she come down the school and confronted the woman. "How can you talk to my son like that?' My mum just cut her off. She was protective of me still even though I was getting into bad habits. From then on Mrs Evans ease up on me.

Like I was still just about keeping up at school but it weren't the main thing on my mind. I was more interested in getting high and getting girls. When I was sat there at my desk I'd be looking at a girt and thinking, cor she's looking nice. My mind would be side tracked away from the books. If I couldn't get any weed at school I'd just go home and hang out on the estate and not even go to school, sitting on one of the walls where we used to hang till 1 or 2 in the morning, smoking weed with my friends. My mum sometimes caught me and would go mad at the negative life I was living and beat the hell out of me. But it didn't stop me. To cover my tracks I forged letters.

Sorry Wayne was late. Wayne's got a bad tummy. He's not feeling good. Wayne wasn't at school. He had to see the doctor. For me school was all about puffing in the toilets and seeing which girl you can get.

I was running all these lads. Some of them arranged a fight for me with this big massive, African bloke called Tufni. He must have been 6ft he started chasing me with a can of coke, and he started fighting and bang bang, I thumped his face and battered him. But he just got up and came at me again. I had respect for him for that. In the evening and at the weekends we took over the spaces under the garages from the older heads. Me and the Gun Posse were now the upcoming young bloods on the estate. We would take candles, drink Guinness, smoke weed and play strip poker with some of the hood rats which was ghetto slang for girls who were up for anything. The aim was to get them butt naked and ask for the rinse. i.e. sex.

There is a pattern to everything, like sewing. It was a pattern that stayed with me all those young times. Weed, Guinness, chill with a girl and then sex. There was a girl called Claudette who would let me feel her up underneath the flats. She was older than me, 14 years old, but she would never let me have sex with her, used to chat to her late at night in a park and she would tell me about girls and how do girls do it and what they liked and it would turn me on. My hands would be going round her like it was nobody's business. But when I dropped her off at home I noticed there was always men outside her house. I don't know whether it was because of what her mum or her dad was into. Her dad's nickname was Mr Parting Head coz he had this enormous center parting.

One time the activities went a bit wrong. If we wanted some privacy, rather than hang out underneath the garages we used to go to a "catch." They were these empty council flats on the estate. We used to kick down the door and use them as hideouts where we could drink, smoke and chill without being bothered. We'd do loads of stuff there, have Subbuteo tournaments there, play cards, smoke weed, plan activities. Sometimes we would have the catch for several months before the council came arid boarded them up or put in new tenants. I was in one of the notches in Crowhurst House with Sadda and Sonn and we each had a girl with us in different rooms. Suddenly from Sonn's room there was the sound of crying. I banged on the door "Sonn, open up." Inside the girl was crying and screaming. "What's going on?" "She bit my thing so I slapped her." "Don't do that to the girl, man. Don't treat her like that." I told him to let her go off home.

Next day I come out of the home with Sonn and Sonn's mum is coming towards us with a man. 'Are you Sonn Nailsmith?" "Yeah." "You are under arrest for indecent assault " As I'm walking back my friends come up to me. "There are news cameras on the estate saying you abducted and raped them girls." 'What are you on about' Don't talk shit." I knew I'd done nothing wrong so I told my mum and brother what had happened, but she started cursing me and hitting me for being involved in that stuff. Then I went round to Sadda's house and all of a sudden police jump out and take me to the police station and start questioning me. They were just listening to rumours so I had to set them straight. "How can anyone abduct three girls in broad daylight?" They carried on questioning me about what had gone on in the other rooms. "I don't know. I can't see through walls. But there weren't no rape."

I knew what had happened. The girls had probably got home late and had invented the rape as an excuse to tell their parents. The whole thing panicked me for a bit but within a few days the police had dropped charges against me. It was a pretty serious thing though, It Stared me and it Stared my mum. But two of my friends went down for it and Sadda got nine months suspended sentence and Sonn got three years. He did the full three years. But it weren't no rape.

My mum told me something that has stayed with me ever since. "You mustn't trust woman. Dey can be bad sometimes." But I thought women was dangerous from then on. I didn't want no commitment with women. I think it messed me up a bit. It's been a little paranoia in me ever since. I never had a stable foundation with woman. Some of my mates had a stable foundation but I never had. I was just playing the field Do you know what I mean?

Our end of the estate near Norton House, Cute house, Bedwell House and Crowhurst House was becoming the central meeting place for all the young ones. I got in with Dandy and his little brother called Forty who was always walking with knives trying to build a name for himself, coz his brother was well known. I'd tease him and he would chase me with knives. But when we clashed I'd always mash him coz he hit like a bitch There was Droy who soon took the street name Star coz one time Mad Up cut him twice dawn the face. There was Star's brother Tug. There were loads of us and it just expanded.

That summer was pretty hot and there were more riots in Brixton. Mum and most of my family members were at a wedding and I took full advantage of her absence. Me and the crew stood on a comer that everyone called Gunman Point near the skateboard park. It had a good view over the Stockwell Road, We joined in the chaos, running around the estate, turning over cars and throwing petrol bombs. I got off on the adrenaline rush. I've always got off on the adrenaline. It inspired me. Things were happening to my body, I had too much energy going on nothing and no one could hold me back. The teenage years were coming and it was like my body was changing. I had a brick in my hand ready to throw it when I saw my mum coming down the road with a big umbrella. I dropped the brick behind a wall. 'What you doin' out here? Don't you see there's a riot going on?" She had a habit of not directly accusing me but knowing what I was up to. She gave me some licks across the back with the umbrella It was one of the last times she hit me. I was getting too big for her. I noticed the hitting suddenly stopped. It was a revelation to me I was too big for her. I felt like I'd become a man. No man can tell me shit. Even though I was only eleven I was big for my age and started following the older boys around.

There was a sound called Sovereign that the older guys were running and at the weekend they would take it to clubs in Stockwell and Loughborough Junction. They were rivals to other sound systems in south London like Coxsone. The Raiders, Mighty Diamonds, Saxon or Hangman. Sometimes there would be a sound clash where rival systems would try and win over the crowd with their music and MCing skills.

We followed Sovereign and at the weekend we'd go to one of their events and get legless on Guinness and brandy. The older guys were like little stars in our community. They were up on stage performing, getting all the girls and all the attention. I'd get envious thoughts. This ain't fair. I want some of that You see I always thought of myself as a leader not a follower. The dances would get pretty crazy. There was often a Yardie man who would fire a gun in the air to salute a tune that Sovereign was playing. One time I was at this dance in Loughborough Road in G Red's house and some Yardies were there and they started saluting the tune and then this big shootout happened and suddenly there was firing all over the place and windows were broken and I was in one of the rooms and had a quick exit. It was Like a Western. So from then it was like the gun rule. When we was in dances and a good tune would come up we would pretend to chip out the ceiling. Bang, bang, bang. Seeing all the attention the guys from Sovereign were getting and the smart dressers who turned up at the club made me hungry. I wanted to get into that life. I envied it and admired it. Even though we was still young we would try and chat up all the girls as they walked past, like we'd seen the older guys do at the dances. We'd stand on Gunman Point, our eyes following them as they came towards us. Then, just as they'd gone past we would say something. "Hey baby, you look good." We mostly got a negative response and we would fly back at them. "Like your shit don't stink," But It didn't stop me dreaming of a life. I began to dream of being a big time gangster with my boys running things, like a little army. But if you don't control your army it can go very bad.

BROADMOOR, 2000

I ain't cried for three years but I cried today. I cried about all the bad things I've done in my life and how I feel about what I've done in my life. I've been hurt by these people and they play games with me and they make me jump through hoops and I've got to abide by their rules and I'm not allowed to argue and I can't dispute or nothing I am powerless. All I want is for them to give me my life back. I just want someone to help me get my life back. I feel hurt by these people. This place has hurt me so much that 1 think I want to harm these people on the streets who put me away. They always giving me hope, hope, hope. Then they tear it down right in front of me and the people in bore, their attitude, their behaviour, you think to yourself! Want to punch that fucker right in the mouth and I want to be super human and I think to myself, how did this go wrong? There's a big, bad man out there, who's been in the genre for twenty years thirty years and he ain't going through what I going through Why am I going through it? I got a girl who I love outside. Shoanna. My brother set me up with her and she visits me from time to time. 1 keep saying to her "keep the faith, keep the faith." But I can't even keep the faith don't know what to do. I'm lost. I'm lost. I'm lost in the system. I was in bed and I wake up and every morning I wake up my education class is canceled. What is that? It's a big fucking game It's a head fuck. What do they want from me? It's better if they shoot me and put me out of my misery. This pain what I'm going through fucked up. All I've done since I've been in the hands of these people is speak the truth. So what do they want from me? To bust their head or chop them up. The world is trucked up. They kick me in the teeth and throw me back down in the pit. The whole fucking lot, the doctors, the staff. I get punished. This place is very connected with authority. Give me a chance to have a life. Give me a fucking job. But they don't give me nothing. They just make me jump through hoops and lie to me. I'm dying, dying. Know what I mean?

AGED 12: POLICE AND THIEVES

All them five pounds and ten pounds I was spending on weed was taking its toll. Feeding our drug habit was costing us. We'd started scoring our own stuff. BP started selling a bit of puff. We used to score our stuff from Jeefy or Muscles, two of the main dealers on the estate. There was also this woman called...I can't remember her name, but she was a Jamaican woman and the main bouncer at the Brixton Academy and his girlfriend also sold ash. Most of the ash was junk but as we got older we smoked sensi which was stronger. Trouble was that ash made you tired and lazy and lethargic and all of that. The amount of money I spent 16 on gear. Terrible. If I had the money in this room on the amount of money I spent on drugs I'd probably fill half of it. Most probably. I'm telling you, I spent a lot of money. I regret it now. That's how we got into crime in a big way. We needed money to buy our drugs. It started with breaking into cars Me and my friends would do the break-ins.

There was this one man on the estate whose car we did, but unfortunately it was Muscles, one of the big guys on the estate, and he knew it was us and came over to the youth center with three man and he called my mate outside and started finger jabbing him. 'You broke my fucking car." "Nah mate, it wasn't me." But Muscles pulled out a length of wire and he started whipping him with the wire, really whipping up, lashing him up until there was blood. I felt sorry for him. But that's what happened if you got Muscle's car But we never got enough money from cars.

It was summer and hot and the crew were hungry and tired of being broke. That's when we would go what we called in them days "drumming." We headed out with screw drivers and coat hangers that we would make into hooks. We'd knock on doors and look through windows and if no one was around we'd use the hook to catch open the window We'd seen the older guys doing it coz we'd been their apprentices. Sometimes we'd get the youngers to slide in a window and open the door for us. Sometimes we would get Papa T just to kick down the door coz he was a big guy and could get into almost any house. Once inside we would raid the contents. We'd take whatever we could. There would be eight of us in there. Like Sadda and Star and Dandy, all squabbling. "I want the TV." "I want the video." "No, I want the video you can have the jewelry." "I don't want no jewelry. I want the video," There was no honour among us coz some of the guys would find cash and only mention it a month later. "Remember that house we did in Stockwell last month, the one with the red door? I found four hundred in cash under the mattress. I ripped you off." Then they'd laugh about it in your face. But they say what goes around comes around. When I got the chance I did the same thing just as much. I'm not proud of all that but as young people growing up in the inner city we felt the odds were against us from the start TVs, videos, passports, gold, money, bank books. Whatever we could get our hands on. We'd do four or five houses a day, just to get money so we can smoke and buy our weed munches and buy clothes and go to parties. We broke so many houses on Stockwell Park estate it was unbelievable. It was a job. We thought of it as earning money. And we needed the new outfits for the next big party. I'd wake up in the morning, link up with Forty or Sadda or a couple of friends "I'm going' robbin' You coming'?" Depending on their reaction you might think, I'm not going with him because he ain't got no bottle. So you might have to turn to someone else. Man dem would want to work with you if you got a reputation of being swift and true or raggo, barefaced it means, you get in there quick and clean, no hesitation and deal with it neatly.

There was a guy called Birdman who was well known and he was good and I liked working with him. There was Couch too but he loved drugs too much and he was greedy. Most times I'd work with Sadda and Star. They were the main men. We learned to steal family allowance books which we could cash a couple of times and then we'd sell them on. Winter was best time coz the lights were off. The residents knew it was us. Sometimes we'd be confronted by people outside their houses and they wanted to beat us up coz they knew it was us but because there were so many of us standing firm we would tell them to fuck off and they'd back down - I never felt sorry for nobody.

Sometimes we'd have to hire a cab to move goods from one place to another to get them sold. We'd just pay off the drivers to keep their mouths shut. That's the life I was leading. Robbing, smoking and going to school. The police turned up one day at school to give some advice about drugs and they told us that all the burglaries going on in the area were just to feed the drugs and it was a habit. I don't know if they knew that the people they were lecturing were the ones causing all the chaos. But it was true we were feeding the habit and just smoking and smoking and robbing to feed the smoking. To tell the truth we didn't think much beyond buying our junk food, looking goad, the latest fashion and the latest trainers. I didn't think beyond that. I just enjoyed it. I was so wrapped up in it that my sister promised to take me to Disneyland, then Jamaica, even Canada to see relatives but I was so wrapped up in the robbing and taking drugs that I didn't want to go. I wanted to stay where I was and break houses. I don't know what was wrong with me. There was a buzz. There's a thing in the belly. An adrenaline buzz. There's nothing like it. It was a fright doing the robberies. You just feel frightened but it's a weird frightened because you are capable of doing it.

There was this one policeman called Duncan and he used to come on the estate and try and catch us and in two years he never got one of us. We'd be on the corner, smoking and hanging on the balconies, getting high before a raid and he would come along and try and catch us out. "I know what you are doing" "Nah, nah. Not doing nuffin' officer." "I'm watching you lot." Sometimes we'd be on the stairways and burning weed and the residents would call the police. But the coppers would cause so much commotion downstairs that we'd hear them before they got to us and get rid of the weed by throwing it off the balcony or in someone's flower pot and by the time the police had puffed their way up the stairs we'd be all smiles.

If nothing was going on that night and we were too tired or cold to go drumming we'd just sometimes be standing on the corner looking for a spontaneous opportunity. When outsiders came to the estate to get a puff we'd be on 'em, and I'd have my hand in their back pocket and someone else with a hand in the front pocket and we'd get money that way.

There was this friend Tank, Muscle's son, who used to get a kick out of beating the punters up. There'd be bare blood. He'd just kick them and punch them. I never intervened even though I thought he was out of order. I was more interested in getting the wallet, sometimes I'd grab the wallet, clear it and be gone and he'd still be beating the man almost to death. After there would be blood on his trainers and on the pavement. Sometimes I'd say something to him as the first kick went in. "What you beating him up for? Concentrate on the money." But he got all excited about it and wouldn't listen to me. I'd leave him be. Fuck it. That's his business. That's what I'd be thinking. I got the cash, sometimes as much as three hundred pounds, to go to chippie and then go raving, so I didn't mind.

The other thing, when man got the money, like I said before it wasn't always honest. There was dishonesty amongst us. After an assault, man who had the wallet would hand it over to share between us. Only sometimes he'd already stole some notes from it. That's the thing about it.

There weren't much honesty in them early days. I wish I hadn't put so much trust in them coz I was storing up trouble for meself in the future. I learnt it too late what was going on. Sometimes in the hours after, I felt sorry when the punters got beaten up bad but mostly I'd put it out of my mind and be gone. We were chased by police loads of times. There'd be chases round the estate with police trying to get us. Birdman, one of our guys, hid in one of those big industrial grey bins that were on the estate all night when the police were searching for him. They never found him. The drugs was just numbness.

We had nothing to eat and we weren't given nothing and we wanted the best clothes and nice trainers so it was like a job. To party, drink and smoke. That's what we wanted and there was nothing to stop us. It's just how it goes. We'd go to Brixton Academy and we'd just jack the crowd. Swatches were in fashion at that time and we'd just take Swatches. And we'd take cash from them and gear and gold. We'd spot our victim, crowd them, back them in a corner and slap them up and get wicked on them. Pull open their coat and go through their pockets and take what they had.

One time we were doing this on the High Street and next minute someone goes to me, "Matty, there's your mum." And we were in the middle of jacking this boy up. So I walked off from it and turned to my mum and picked up her shopping and helped her home with it. I don't know if she knew what we were doing but she never said nothing. Sometimes we'd be walking down Brixton on a hot sunny day after smoking so much drugs that you'd have to eat out immediately. I'd be so hungry that my belly would be touching my back. If we had money we would go for Chinese, Indian or Italians, But most of the time we didn't have money and we'd have to get it. We'd spot a 22 jewellery like a big chain and we had to take it in turns to snatch it. I'd run up, snatch it off someone's neck run down a couple of back streets and I'd have reversible jacket on so I'd reverse it and start walking and jump on train to Hatton Gardens. I'd get eight pounds for a gramme of 22 karat, six pounds for 18 and four pounds for 9. If it was 9 karat you wouldn't bother going to Hatton Gardens, you'd go round the corner to Johnnie's, this shop in the arcade who'd buy it no questions. The most profitable time was Carnival time. That's where it all went down. We would come from the south and head into the west to Notting Hill and just march through the crowd each with his own shot of making a Seller. We'd be selling fake drugs to the punters grabbing chains, pick pocketing, grabbing camcorders -

It was a free for all there were thieves all over the estate. Each one looking to make a fast buck. Like DE. We used to call him cus, but he wasn't really a cousin. He worked at Dominos pizza in Clapham Junction. He had a moped and he used to let me ride it about. Sometimes he would bring me a pizza with pineapple and beef and cheese. That was my favourite. He told me about a plan to rob the Dominos. He gave the combination of the safe to one of his friends who managed to open the safe. They pretended it was an outside job but he wasn't careful enough and got arrested for it. There was also this G, a gangster friend called Lung. He was a gambler. He used to bet on horses Sometimes he would go down the bookies with £5 or £50 pounds. If he made some money I'd try and persuade him to leave it "Come on, let's go.' But he'd stay. Sometimes he'd win 1.000 and I'd say it again. "You've made enough let's go now "No, one more." Then he'd stay and lose the lot.

Sometime I'd be with him and he was so high that he was fearless. "I'm going down to Paddington to creep the Arabs." I'd want to go with him. "Let me come. I can help you out "But he never would bring me down there "I'll see you in the morning." My sister had moved out by this time so sometimes I'd stay at my sisters in the front room sleeping and just as the sun was rising he would come and knock on the door arid lay down bags of alcohol, tobacco and cash that he'd cleared from the Arabs. Then he would go off and gamble it all away. He was a friend. A few years older than me. But d'you get me? The lifestyle was all addictive.

My mum must have suspected something now coz I was wearing good clothes and new trainers and she never gave me enough money to keep buying new clothes and trainers. Where 'you get dem trainers?" "I been bricklaying mum." To keep my mum off my back I would tell her I been doing jobs and working on a friend's dad's allotment. But there was this friend of my mum who was always grassing me up to my mum telling her we were in Brixton and teefing boys. "You gotta control dat boy of yours coz he's a bad man in the making." Nothing was going to stop me though. I had the hunger. I wanted more. From burglary it just escalated. My mind was telling me to go up a stage. I'll step up into something different That's why I got into dealing drugs on the road it weren't a hard choice. It was a natural progression It started off small. I'd wake up in the morning and need to go out there and do something. Sometimes I'd think, I'm gonna make a raise. Instead of going to school I'd buy an ounce, cut it up into bits and in the evenings go to clubs and sell it. It was acid in them days. But I didn't make much money coz I ended up smoking the profit. It was all about getting high. But 1 discovered a new drug. I discovered that you could make a lot of money from it Maybe I could have stopped things at this point. Maybe I could have taken a different path. But probably not coz it was just natural. I got mixed up with crack and got my first gun. 13 years old.

BROADMOOR, 2000

I been seven years in the Big B now. Do I know myself better? Do I know Matty? Has generous, caring, sensitive. Got a bad side to him though too. Don't like being betrayed. Don't like being taken for fool and with that bad side comes action sometimes what one regrets. That's about if. Is he controllable? Yeah course.

Here seven years and I ain't even had five fights...Well ain't even had ten fights. Say ten. Ten fights in seven years. When I was outside years ago that would be ten fights in a week. Ten in a week. So that shows some control there don't it? Totally different person. I'm trying to get off this ward but all they want to do is give me drugs and tell me I'm ill. I'm trying to change but they want me to come out of this place in the wrong way you get me? I don't know what is going to happen to me man.

I've tried to deal with mankind but mankind has got a different agenda. Some are out to kill you, some are out to earn off you, some are out to abuse you. Some are out to use you. As I've been growing up I've always had this knowledge of trying to divert from things and seeing to things but there never been in a situation like this in my life where I feel so helpless like my life don't mean shit. Know what I mean? That's how I feel. And I'm praying to God, praying to him now.

Why is he doing this to me? What does he want me to do? He ain't intending nuttin'. I'm so wrapped up and seated in my own way of life that maybe it's too hard for God to find me find God. I find God But 1 don't know if he wants to find me. There are these forces in these places trying to lead you astray and you have to fight them. I don't think God wants to help me. I'm suffering. This pain over all these years and this pain ain't going nowhere, It's hard to change me being in these ways. All they say to me is I'm ill What the fuck is going on? How can I be so unfunctioned? I don't know if I'm going or coming. I feel like I've been lied to, abused, taken for a ride. It seems too real. You know what I mean?

AGED 13: CRACK AND GUNS

It was CT who introduced me to crack. CT was a friend from school and one day we were in Myatt's Field and he comes up to me. "Guess what. I robbed thirty stones from a Yardie." At that time I was only smoking weed. "You smoke. I ain't smoking man." 20 But I was tempted. I rolled a spliff. "But a little bit in the weed for me." He did and I started smoking. It was sweet. The two of us smoked all thirty rocks. We went back to school. He fell asleep at his desk and I sat there, completely off my head, writing a fantastic story.

Of course I knew about crack before that. There was this man called Cheeks who lived on Balfour Road opposite the Brixton Academy who tried to get the younger boys hooked on crack as a way of getting the youths dependent on him. He'd stand by a cash point on the High Street and signal to one of the younger boys who would steal the cash from the punter. Then they'd meet round a corner and he'd buy some rocks to give to the younger kid. Then they'd go on another move and the younger kid would be a lookout and the same thing would happen. He'd make the little kids crack addicts by feeding them crack. At the time I didn't realise what he was doing and there were times later when I'd do jobs for him but mainly I stayed clear.

My brothers and sister had kept an eye on me. But when they all moved out of the house I was left living alone with my mum and there were less people to keep an eye on me. Star had been smoking for some time and he roped us into this new cotch round the corner from Magoo's house on the other side of the estate. Dandy and his best friend Martin had set up to sell crack there and we was a place were we could hang and be private, on the other side of the estate. It's where we stored stolen goods and it became our base. Me and Star and Forty and Billion used to go in there and help chop up the crack. I had butterflies in my stomach when I first smoked it. I didn't used to inhale it properly. I'd suck it in and breathe it out straight away. I didn't like the stuff. I preferred weed. It was only later that I got hooked on it. It was a simple path from smoking weed to selling crack.

Like I said I used to sell a few bags of weed just enough to keep me in my own supply, but there was a need to do more and get bigger. It was the influx of Yardies on the estates that changed the drug game. Crack became a big thing in our area around Somerleyton. Fiveways, Loughborough, Myatt's Fields. There was a house on Lawn Road where me and the crew bought weed and two stones of crack and we'd go to these clubs and there was the real high life We'd go there and smoke the stones and drink champagne and brandy. But we were always walking from place to place. Even in the rain. We had no wheels. We were always walking. That's when we started to see these Yardies men in Mercs and BMWs driving around the estates. That's when it clicked and I turned to my mates "Are we idiots or something? Them Yardies are in bare Mercs and we are walking around in the rain. That's not right." That's when I realised that there was money to be made selling crack One day one of the older guys I used to cut the crack for goes to me. "Do you want to help us?" That's how I started properly on the road.

The estate is a 24 hour place full of shady characters In the day the mums and kids are out. But at night a whole other list of characters come out doing their stuff. Drug dealers, prostitutes, burglars. They come out at night and sleep in the day. But my mum always used to tell me the same thing, the early bird that catches the worm." And that's how I started to run my life. I would wake up at four a.m. go round to some of the older heads like Dandy to get my shit. He would give me a little eight ball, that's an eighth of crack for two hundred pounds on consignment. Then we'd all meet up at Fiveways near the Green Man pub, a place at Loughbrough Junction that had five roads leading off it. I'd Cut the eight into pieces and sell it for six hundred pounds.

I'd be out there all morning, serving people on the road, jumping in cars, jumping out of the cars and at about ten in the morning, if the inclination got me. I'd put the cash away and go to school, making excuses why I was late. The very first time I was dealing though I learnt my first big lesson about crack dealing. It was my first time out on the road and i never forgot it. I was on Raton road. This car drive up and a head went out the window. "Give me three stones quick. Police are coming." I spat them out of my mouth and he handed over what I thought was money. But when I found out it was just paper not money I got so mad and dived through the car window and grabbed the gear stick and when they tried to drive off it was going in and out of gear down the road and my legs are hanging out of the window and kept hitting the parked cars so I jumped in the car through into the back seat "Give me my kicking money. Don't fuck about with me.' 'We will give you your money. Alright mate we will give it you." They took me to Camberwell, the hack streets of Camberwell and stopped in front of the police station. "See our radio we are police now fuck off, it's a tax." I looked at the radio and it didn't look like a police radio to me. "That's a cab radio. That ain't no police radio. You're no police." Well I thought about thumping them and making a scene but we were right outside the police station arid I didn't want to risk being arrested so I jumped out of the car and caught a cab back and all the other dealers were all laughing at me. And I was furious. It was my first day on the line and I got stung. Then I realised the crack game wasn't as easy as all that.

You gotta be alive. That's why crack dealers smoke to be alive, you have to be on your toes. You have to keep the instinct going. It went on like that for months. It was a whole early morning drama out there. Coz we were so young, we'd be a hit of a feature for the customers who went on about how young we were.

There'd be Yardies, Angell Town boys. English people, all of us dealing. The competition was pretty fierce but there would be enough for everyone to eat. Sometimes the Yardies would come up to me when they'd got rid of all their stuff. "Yeah man, give me a stone." And sometimes I'd give 'em a stone and they would give another one back to me later, But they'd also send customers to me. That's how I found business by getting on with the big players like Mad Max. By about eight in the morning I'd be really tired so I'd start smoking coke to keep me awake and make me lively. "Let's get a morning coffee' That was our word for it. Having some cocaine in the morning. Because its a 24 hour game. It never sleeps, You gotta be on the job 24/7.

Sometimes we were so tired on the road, arguing and standing there coz you had to do a lot of arguing coz some people would come and try and swap your good stuff with bad stuff. And sometimes we'd hand over some foil but all it contained was candle wax so they'd come back and complain and you'd have to beat them up. There was also this woman called Pep who all the time she was selling fake work. She was always dressed sharp and always out there but she was shoplifting her clothes which was how she looked sharp. She was always busy with cars coming from everywhere and it took me ages to realise she was selling fake stuff. To try and make it more open we started selling it in cling film. Before us everyone used to sell it in foil but we came up with the idea of selling it in cling-film because you could see the tings and knew they couldn't sting you.

So we set the standard. Still, there were always stings. I was with Birdman on the frontline when a car drove up and the window opened. "Quick give us two stones." The the car drove off leaving Birdman open mouthed. But the car turned round and came back. The window opened again. "You thought I was gonna sting you init Birdman pretended to be all cool, "No. I knew you were going to pay." "Yeah. Well don't worry man, I'm gonna pay you. Give us another three stones." So Birdman gives them another three stones and the car drives off quickly again. And the guys in the back of the car are laughing at him because we never seen them again. To be honest we were laughing at him too. There were always scams and arguments and drama, fights and gunshots, all kind of tings. There was this guy called Ba who when he smoked and finished all his shit he would come on the line with an Uzi. He'd be desperate for some crack and he would go up to a dealer and point his Uzi at them. 'Give me your rocks.' 'I ain't got none." "Strip and show me. Strip. Strip.' They'd have to drop their pants and cover their balls and everything. And he would find their shit and make them give to him. We were all wary of him. I was wary of him. He come for me one time and he tried to take drugs off me. I couldn't fight a man with an Uzi so 1 just give it to him. He just come on to me. What else could I do?

There were loads of prostitutes there too coz crack and prostitutes go hand in hand. They always pestered us for rocks in exchange for sex but I wanted my twenty so I wouldn't do it. But I had a few friends who would go with the prostitutes for a few hours and for a few stones they would get a bit of sex. Sadda was the main culprit. He was always going off for a blow job. But the prostitutes were okay. They got clients for us. Having them around was good business. They were nice people and sometimes you'd see them in a right state, clucking and all that and you'd give them something. There was this woman called Suzie Wong, she escaped from Holloway and she was on the run and selling herself in Fiveways. She was a nice girl, and she would come up to me on the road and whisper in my ears. "I'll give you a blow job for a stone.' "No, I deal cash ' She'd pick up one of the stones I'd left on the floor and plead with me. "Come on. A blow job for this. Two blow jobs. - That's when I'd lay down the law coz I didn't want her touching me gear. "Give it back or I'll I beat your kid up.' So she gave it back and walked off in a huff. Sometimes it was a comical scene us all on the corner selling crack. It was a hundred metre dash to the block. Sometimes the police would drive down the road, turn round, turn on their lights and hit the block. I was running and it was in slow motion and there was adrenaline going through me and I was running as fast as I could and most of the times I just got into the estate. It was always as if it was in slow motion. I guess it was the adrenaline that made it feel like that. The older smokers loved it when the police came because all the dealers would throw their works in the grass to avoid being caught and, once the police had gone, the older smokers would arrive with their eyes always fixed on the floor looking for rocks that had been left behind. There was a tall, old man granddad guy whose name was Slygo and as soon as the police disappeared he'd be out there, his eyes fixed on the floor looking for rocks muttering to himself in Jamaican. He never found much but he was harmless enough and we would give him a smoke every now and then. And I'd just be running around, jumping in cars making money, going to school and being back there the next day. When we were too tired from all the crack dealing we went to Marston House in Angell Town where this prostitute Pauline had a catch, an empty flat that the council hadn't taken back. We just used to hang out in there smoking weed and chatting, If I didn't want to go to school I'd just hang there and Pauline used to bring all the prostitutes in and they'd be offering us sex and piping and asking for a spliff but I'd just sell it to them. I didn't want nothing from them. I didn't want the sex. I preferred the cash. It was all pretty crazy. And dangerous. Which is why I bought a gun. It was protection If someone messed around with you, you could shoot them. Growing up on the streets like that you have to revert to negative tactics. If you had a gun, they knew you had a gun. They wouldn't mess with you A few weeks before a friend who lived on the estate showed me his collection of guns. "Do you want to buy one?" "Yeah OK He offered me a single barrel shotgun. I liked it. It was slim and easy to pull apart, I gave him £50 and he asked me to meet him on a corner of the estate that night. I met him, put it under my jacket, went home, broke it down and hid bits of it in different places. 13 years old and I'd become a gunman. And within a few days I'd need it.

BROADMOOR, 2001

I relapsed the other day. They said I relapsed and upped my medication. They said 1 was like a dog. I ain't been taking drugs. They upped my medication from ten to twenty. Just more sleep. Sleeping more. 1 know it's not madness. It's real. I wasn't psychotic. Something that came over me and made me do those things. Like I said it's called the blood sport game. Billboard signs telling me who to rob and all of that, it was real. Is that a gift or a curse? I don't know. It's the madness. They keep telling me I'm mad for some reason. I don't know why. So, what if I was out there not at liberty on the streets? What would I be doin'? Will the voices come again and tell me to kill myself. No, PH be out there on the streets playing the game. Playing the game Playing the game Meeting people, dealing with them. I'm trying to put my thoughts into perspective and get them correct. The spirits protected me for so long. My illness is that think I'm a dog and that the system is controlling me. That's what the psychiatrist says, it's madness.

AGED 14: GUNMAN POINT

I was in Angell Town, not far from Fiveways and one of the dealers whose street name was Fire goes to me, "Ernie wants half a sixth of crack." Ernie was this friend of Fires so I was happy to help out, "I'll sort him out." So I walked down to where Ernie was and gave him the crack through the window and the wheels start spinning and he drives off. And I'm trying to hold onto the car. "Hey you fucker, come back. Give me my stuff back." I was like, t wonder if he set me up. I thought I'd watch out for him. And I get to the corner of the estate and I see Fire jumping into Ernie's car at the traffic lights. That's when I realised that the two were working together to rip me off. The fucker he set me up. So next day I was back on the corner and I confronted Fire. "I don't like the way you set me up man." 'What do you mean?" "I never set you up" "Don't fucking lie to me." Then he pulls out a knife on me, like a normal dinner knife and tries to stab me. So we start fighting and he pulls my jacket off me as we are fighting and rips my trousers. So I kick out at him and he falls down the steps and runs off through the garages. But as I try to chase him my trousers are all ripped and I can't run properly. But he's still got my jacket on me which is where all the crack is so I shout after him, "Give me my jacket." So he dropped my jacket. I picked up my jacket and dusted it down and checked the pockets and all the crack had gone. You're trying to rob me. Right star, I'm gonna blaze you up.

So I went home to get my one pop, the single barreled shotgun. This is the first time that I'm gonna use it. But it's not where I left it and I looked everywhere for it but couldn't find it so I picked up a big kitchen knife and went hack on the line, and see Mad Max and told him what Fire had done. So Mad Max tells me that he knows where Fire is and that he's round this girl's house. So we go there and Mad Max goes in and tells me to wait there. Anyway he doesn't come out for ages and when he does come out he tells me that Fire isn't there. I know there's something dodgy going on but I think to myself, fair enough, I'm gonna sort it out another time.

About three months later I see Fire in a convertible Peugeot and I squared up to him. "I don't like what you done, you know: "Sorry man I was clucking that day. I was desperate for drugs. I really needed it." He gave me some money for the rocks and apologised. I left it at that. I let it go. But when I saw my mum I asked her about the gun. "Have you seen the metal pole I keep in the wardrobe?" I'd broken it down from the barrel so she wouldn't know what it was. "I ain't seen it. What it is?" "It's just a metal pole morn, it's nothing. It don't do no harm." "Oh." Anyway, I never seen it again. Never. I always wonder what happened to that one pup. The thing was, t still never seemed to have enough money. The money from the selling game never added up. I never had much financial responsibilities but I was wild with my money and spent it on drugs and clothes. I used to give a small amount of change to my mum but not enough. Now I feel bad that I didn't give her more. I smoked more than I should or I went raving and burned some, burning it out with bare people. But I always had to give the man dem their consignment money and one day I owed £250 and I was thinking boy, better give em back their money. Coz you were never sure of the consequences of not paying.

Luckily I found some money under my mattress, paid them and got the next one on consignment and got back out of debt. But next week I'd be back in debt again. That's why it was a real commitment being on the road. You had to be real committed and persistent to keep the business going 24/7, rain or shine. And it was a commitment to a way of life that just dragged you deeper and deeper into it. And the thing is that you hardly knew how low you were sinking.

BROADMOOR, 2001

Waiting for the review is driving me mad. Coming up, coming up, always coming up. I might have been badder outside doing bad things, but I feel more disturbed than what I was then. At that time it's what was real, what was going on, but at least i was free. In this situation I've got no control. No. I can't do nothing. I'm dictated to all the time and I just got to sit down and can't do nothing. And what the fuck am I doing sitting down doing nothing? They've canceled my classes because I refused to team carpentry. It was like the slave trade. I'm an entrepreneur. Back in the day I was finding some way of surviving. I could do something in them days. That's why I cant sit here doing nothing. That's why I can't sit it out. That's when I don't give a fuck. I'm in an angry state of mind. There are all these lawyers who come and see me. I get to realise solicitors are bastards. They sit on the fence. Where does that leave me? Rejection and neglection.

I've got athlete's foot. I'm falling apart. Another chapter of my past is coming to me. It's like a vibe reminiscing. It's how you mold into this life. That's all there is. That's all you are brought up with. You have your life that you are born with and you mold into it that way.

AGED 15: KIDULTHOOD

I was still going to school but I never paid much attention. My attention was not what it should have been. I was mare interested in trainers than in maths. One time 1 had an argument with Vin at school. He was a year younger than me and he baited me. "You are a tramp. I'm gonna get my new ZX 5000 Adidas trainers when I come to school next week." "No, you're the tramp. I'm gonna get my new 7000." But I had no money so me and the crew went and cleared this bloke's house out on Stockwell park estate. It was pretty good coz he had a brand new washing machine and he had a brand new gameboard and video We cleared the house out and my cousin said, "You can have the video for yourself." So I took the video, hid it in a cupboard coz I didn't want anyone to take it. It was around New Years and I said to my friends. "No one is going to rip me off this year and if they do watch what happens to them. They are going to pay." I'd been ripped off a few times before from other people so I felt I had to stand up to people. "No one will take liberties with me this year." Anyway, my sister's boyfriend, Blow, came round one day when I weren't there and took the video. I was furious. I confronted my sister. "Where does he live?" He'd taken liberties so I wanted to pay him back. Me and a friend called Royle jumped on a bus with my sister towards Streatham. I'd taken a Southern Comfort bottle and filled it with stones in the bottom and petrol and put a sock over the top. Nobody could see I had it in my hand but it still made the bus stink of petrol. My sister pointed out his house. "That's where he lives. Right there "I got off the bus. My first thought was to throw the bottle at the house but there was an old woman downstairs and I thought it might kill her because she might not be able to get out in time. I had to revise my plan. 'Where's his car?" My sister pointed out his car Forty went up to it and smashed the window I lit the bottle and threw it in and we all ran. By the time got to the bottom of the road... Boom.

The whole thing went up in the air and burn out. We ran away down the street. We needed an exit plan me and my sister. Come round to my friend's house. We'll hide out there for a bit." My sister though wanted to go back and see what had happened. "No, I'm gonna pretend that I didn't know nothing about it and go back down there all innocent." A few days later, my sister comes and tells me that Blow is on to me and reckons that she was one of the only people who knew which one was his car so he was blaming her. There were four of us playing Nintendo at my sister's house with my nephew when he knocked on the door. Before I opened it I put a big kitchen knife down the pants. He came in with his brother Tally. "I want to speak to you." "If you want to speak to me, talk to me in here 'star." "No I want to talk to you in private." "No I'm not coming out." Anyway, he told my friends to get out the room and he goes to me. Who burnt my car?" "I don't know nothing. What you asking me for?" "That was my car 'star." "1 know nothing about it." Anyway his mobile phone rings and they left. But that wasn't the end of it. I went to the funfair with Sadda and Mark and we were on our way back and my sister's house was in darkness. I'm thinking, this is --strange. I knocked on the door and eventually Big D my nephew opened the door and he looked shaken. "What's the matter with you?" We walked in. "Where is the stereo? Where is the video?" The place was a tip. Big D was crying. "Blow, Kevin and Royle came" They had terrorised everyone They had taken the TV, stereo, video and slashed the sofa. So me and my friends went round to my mum's and drop Big D off. We needed to talk things over. "How are we going to deal with it?" 'We are gonna kill them and fuck them up." I had my knife still and as I'm walking back to my sister's I see Royle. So I go up to him and confront him. "How can you attack my sister and take her stuff?" `They put my hand over a boiling kettle. They tortured me. They made me do it. Blow and Kevin made me do it." "What you did was family. This is personal now." I pulled out my knife and stabbed him in the leg and he collapsed. There was blood rushing everywhere. I thought, fuck this. And my friends were a bit freaked and ran off to the other side of the estate coz they thought I'd killed him. They went talking to everyone_ Wally's turned mad. He's killed Royle." I called an ambulance and gave them the address. "There's a guy bleeding on the landing." Then I went to my brother's house and told him that they'd wrecked our sister's flat. So the two of us went on the rampage looking for Blow. He weren't in so we went to his brother's house, Kevin, and he weren't in but his brother Wayne was in and we terrorised him. We were going to throw him off the landing, but we took his video and stereo and cut up his bed and took the stereo back to my sister's. But the police are now looking for me coz someone was stabbed on Stockwell Park estate and the police were looking for the person who'd caused the damage. Someone lost pints of blood and all that. So I stayed at my brother's. By Monday police raided my mum's house. And she told them where I was. The night before I was puffing loads of ash with my brother and Yann and he said give me the knife and take mine coz you don't want to be caught with the suspect weapon so we swapped it. He left and I sat there sleeping in the chair. Anyway, my little nephew who was four years old suddenly shouted out. 'Look police are coming." I looked out the window and saw police running into the house, So I quickly hid the drugs and the weapons and woke everyone up and put a cigarette in my mouth to look all casual. They boxed it out of my mouth but they couldn't find the drugs coz I'd cheeked them up my ass. So we got arrested then and there. "No comment." That's what I kept saying when they asked me if I'd stabbed Royle. They kept me over night and I had a Off while they told me that it was serious and that we were going to court the next day for attempted murder. But the next day they dropped charges against my brother and dropped my charge to Section 18. GBH with intent. The solicitor said I was looking at 7 years. But in court I told them about Royle's past activities. I didn't expect Royle to turn up in court but he did. All that defending myself I'd done as a kid during the Reject Book game came in handy, "Your honour how can you believe a man like this? He's a thief and he stole a bus "And it was true, A few months earlier, amongst many of the crimes he'd done he'd stolen a bus that was parked up by the Brixton Academy and crashed it in Brixton. "Did you steal a bus?" "Yes, I stole a bus your honour." The judge summarized the case and after consulting various papers told the jury the witness wasn't reliable so the charges were dropped. And as for Blow and Kevin who'd started the whole thing they could hardly look at me again. Hey I didn't want no argument no more. We'd made our point coz we never heard much talk from them again and the beef with Blow and Kevin just fades down. See that's how it was, using terror on the estate.

BROADMOOR, 2001

People hurt me and they done something to me in my life and I don't know what they done. I smoked weed but what the fuck have they done to me? I'm some scientific modification of something I'm an experiment. I feel like I'm an experiment. I want to stay away from people. This whole thing I'm going through since I was 19, they've done something to me. They've made me act this way This is what I wanna ask them: "Why are you doing this to me?" And I hear voices in my head answering back. "Because you are a right piece of shit.' That's when t end up thinking a lot and tormenting myself. What is going on? What is really going on? Can't work it out. I hear all these funny vibes, homosexual thoughts. Where is all this coming from? Where's God? Maybe someone sold my soul or something. I don't know what they done to me. I don't like what they are trying to turn me into Deranged pervert. They can succeed in anything they want to do. The nurses said "you frighten us.. "Everyone's illness is different. A nurse said this is one of the oldest institutes in Great Britain and she frightened me. I am suffering from nightmares I'm 27 in December and my life has got no better.

AGED 16: CREEPING

To supplement the crack dealing and keep out of debt I carried on with the house burglaries. We moved onto bigger richer homes. We started doing hundreds of break-ins. You needed to do it coz you needed to have good clothes. If you never had them garms you would be treated like a nobody. We were all into our garms and we'd be going up to the West End to buy designer labels like Chevignon, Nat Naf, Week and Best Company, Chippies, No garms meant you had no game. I'm remembering about all the burglaries we used to do. How we used to operate on the estates all around the area and how we got to do houses and steal antiques in all those yuppies areas.

In and around Brixton it started getting yuppified. The vibe in the smart areas was changing as people got money and started buying antiques and stuff. We saw it as a money-making opportunity. It was a new way of making paper. We got really into it. We'd go to auctions and find out about paintings and all kinds of stuff. We realised how much money all this old antique stuff was selling for Yeah. I'm gonna get a bit of that. How would it start? There would be me and Forty. Stripes, Debe. Sadda, YupBoy. We'd be round my sister's house, really high coz we'd been smoking it would be in the middle of the night. "Let's go creeping." We'd be so high that we'd all be up for it We'd drive round to the richer parts of town in Kennington or Dulwich and we'd break into someone's house while they were sleeping. Someone would stand watch and we'd jimmy open the door or a window. We'd creep up into the bedroom. Sometimes they'd be in bed, steeping. It wouldn't stop us. We'd steal jewelry, cash books, bank cards, pin numbers and clear out the house. We were brazen. Once we were creeping this house belonging to a nurse and we got in the bedroom and there was this nurse and a man was shagging her. She saw us and I don't know whether she was so Stared or what but she just stared at us with big eyes as we were creeping the house. She just lay there on her back and we just watched this man shag this woman and he feel asleep and she just lay there watching us until we went out the house.

29 We always made our way back to my sister's with the loot. At my sister's place there were locks and locks on the door to keep police and the uninvited out. We would make a helluva noise getting back in there and she would wake up. "What are you doing?" We'd just stash the stuff in the house and go and sell it the next day, using cab drivers that we paid off. When we'd made the money we buy some champagne, a new outfit, a little bit of money saved. That's what it was about. It was a game to us. We'd be so high that we wouldn't care. It didn't always go smooth and there was a lot of mistrust amongst us. There was this one creep I did with, Star and Sadda. I was in the bedroom going through the wardrobes and I pulled out this drawer and there was loads of jewellery inside and I got all excited about how much was in it. My plan was to empty it all in my pocket but as I pulled out the drawer I dropped it and it all fell out it made such a noise that the man woke up. "Who's there? What's going on?" The man must have been terrorised. I run to the door and got to the garden and there was a wall and a jump to the street. I got on the wall and below me were some pillars that stop you parking your car.

Anyway I messed up a bit and before I jumped I fell over the wall upside down and my keys fell out my pocket into the man's garden. So there was I on one side of the wall with the keys on the other and this man was now at the window shouting and screaming. I was in a precarious position. Fuck, I can't leave without my keys he might chase them down. I figured the guy was frighten as much as I was so I jumped back into the garden and picked up my keys. Sadda, Mark, me and Star all met up afterwards to show what we'd got and divided it up, but I must have missed something because Mark, who was lookout, told us later that Star had found £450 in cash which he'd kept from us. But what goes around comes around. Because me and Sadda hadn't told Star that we got the cash-card and the pin number from that same robbery. We thought fair enough we are pulling out money every week, so you bastard, fair enough. There was no honour among thieves. We didn't really stop to think about what we were doing or about the victims. All I knew was that if someone came to my house to steal I'd pick up a baseball bat and knife and chop them up.

I was a victim of crime once. Someone broke into my car and stole my mobile phone and radio. I was in Croydon, There were some older men hanging around and I was sure it was them. "Do you think you can rob me. I'm gonna bash you." It was the wrong thing to say. Their eyes lit up. They could tell that I was a dealer and they knew they were going to pipe me. And so I started to run.

Usually when someone is chasing me I can shake them off but they were thinking we're piping crack tonight. And I was running and running and going through cars, all over the place and everytime I looked behind me they were there running after me. They were big black guys. I ran into this posh hotel with porters and I pushed people carrying plates of food and drinks and knocked everyone over as they all tried to scatter. I got to the lift and banged on the button but by the time I'd turned round they had me. They tore off my jacket, had hands all over me and took my shit, my knife and throwed me a fiver back. I walked out of the place but I was pretty stirred up. I said to myself I'm gonna turn this place into fireworks. Everyone on the line was watching me as I walked away and shouted at the guys who'd done it. "Do you think you are going to get away with that?" My cousin was there and he calmed me down. I smoked some crack and felt better after that. I was so angry I saw this girl and I bring her to some squat and start to fuck her and then she starts saying she loves me and wants to be with me and I thought, you don't love ma, you sleep with everyone. So I go away and I left her crying and went about my business. The ting is I was really harsh with women. My mind was so full of myself that there were never room for anyone else.

BROADMOOR, 2001

After being in this place for so long, the love that I have for people outside is slowly dying. Because they don't show me no love so there is bare hating. There is anger for the disrespect they show me. It's coming to the point where if I get outside, I will play it on my terms and take 'em out coz I've had enough, I've had enough. People are fucking up my life. Now can you be in the game outside and not confront me about it? What kind of fucked up shit is that? This place ain't curing me, it's making me insane. Madness 24/7.

It's making me nuts. There comes a point where I break. I don't know what they want from me I will hurt someone soon I'm telling you. I can't handle this shit. It's madness. I can't take it no more and they banned me from school for the biscuit business. I blocked the teacher's way. She says she felt threatened. Fucking mad. Fucking barmy place. I will tear someone's fucking heart out. I've tired chilling out and it doesn't work. I'm not playing this game no more. I've had enough. That's all I'm saying. I be and look for the hope But it's hard to find hope when you're not even sure it's there.

AGED 16 (cont'd): BUSINESS MAN

The ting about the drug business is that it ain't easy You don't become a major drug dealer overnight. You have to put work into it — you know what I mean? So I was always looking for new business. I was hanging out at Gunman Point with two girls called Dom and Joanna when Star arrived with some heroin I thought this might be something to add to the crack dealing. "Matty, I've got a sixth of brown. What shall I do with it?" None of us
really knew coz we were not into heroin. I'd smoked it twice but it made me itch and I didn't even know I was smoking it. Someone had mixed it in ash and I just smoked it, I never liked the stuff. That's down and out business. Coke is the rich life, the high life. It's more attractive. But even coke I didn't snort. I used to smoke it. Never piped it before neither. But it will always get you. Heroin, crack. Eventually you get addicted even to the

spliff. Anyway I carried the brown home and talked to my brother about it. "You know man you can make lots of money from that. You gotta bag it up? He told me to go to McDonalds and gel a plastic spoon and use it to bag up the heroin. It seemed like a good idea. I bagged it up in little wraps and went to Billion's patch. He was one of the older heads who'd been sent to prison for shooting Big D. He was always a notorious guy when I was growing up but suddenly now he was out and he'd set up a crack dealing base and heroin den in one of the flats in Borough House and he had lots of people coming to see him. So I stood there, freezing my balls off, with my nose running and my feet numb waiting to intercept his punters. "Do you want to buy some brown?" 'No, sorry mate. I'm goin' to see Billion." "But look man, I got a good packet here." They'd get all inquisitive and by the end of the day I'd managed to take about three hundred pounds. We started selling heroin to everyone. Students were the best customers. It weren't easy to get customers. Some of the heroin customers were beggars and real down and outs. Some were workers and some criminals. I never went down the heroin road. I'd seen what people looked like. Them people looked like the living dead. They were like zombies always sick in the morning. But it didn't stop me selling and gradually we started to steal Billion's customers.

Hanging out on Fiveways dealing crack became less appealing after that. Dealing for yourself. That was where my future lay. It was Billion who suggested it. "Do you want to go into business on the lines?" I got a mobile phone and with Billion's help I set up business for myself. So now I was getting my own clients and the phone starts to ring and this little business starts to go well. I went into partnership with Smite and with Seller and people would ring us and we would go and deliver racks and bags of B. Business was going so well that we'd hire a rental every week and drive around all day delivering the drugs all over London. I gave myself a dealing name, Blue, coz I used to wear blue and it sounded good. Blue You. So we set off in the car and Sollar was always moaning at me but it was constructive moaning. "Stop smoking weed while you're driving." "Concentrate on the business." "You can't just drive around all day smoking we gotta make some £s" "If you wanna smoke then wait till we get back to base." To be honest, it was doing me head in. I didn't want nobody tellin me nuttin. I didn't want no dictating or moaning coz I got plenty of that when I got home.

My mum had begun to notice a change in my behaviour If I got back late at night after a day burning my mum would be waiting for me. "Look at your eyes. Day all red. Dee weed drunk your brain. You're a mash up "Her voice would be like razor blades to me. It would be like razor blades and depending how stoned I was I would stagger to my room trying to get her to stop hassling me. "Leave me alone mum." I'd bolt the door and lie down on the bed and me head would be bursting to some tune we just got from Jamaica. And she would be at the door still cussing me. "Your mind is like a sheep with no master." I hear it all but it hurt my head. That was my mum. It didn't seem as though she knew what was going on but she was watching everything. I took a job making furniture one time to try and make a go of it and make her happy. It was a carpentry place in Balham. Cash in hand. £400 a week. Seven days a week. But I was too hot headed as a youngster and the men that ran the place used to get me running around doing all the carrying and fetching rather than let me make something. I didn't like the way they talked to me so I walked out after two months. Then I tried to get an apprenticeship at engineering companies like Bosch. But all the placements fell through and t go t disheartened. That's when I went back to the streets. That was my mistake In the morning though I'd be up and out of the house. I had to keep working coz It was big business.

I was always up first thing and out till late at night. I had no peace whatsoever because I was in great demand for drugs. I was in bed sleeping and trying to chill and they'd be throwing stones at my window. They'd be coming to me "Blue. Got any B?' "Blue. Give me three rocks." Non-stop it was. That's how much in demand. It got to the point where we were taking so many calls on the phone that I had guys delivering the gear on bikes and mopes. It was like home delivery. We were making nine hundred pounds a day but it was hard work from eight in morning till ten at night and then sometimes I would go right on through the night. The drugs was keeping me awake I was taking crack and Star was taking crack and Sollar was taking crack and we were driving around all night delivering drugs and sometimes hanging out at Fiveways drumming up business and meeting friends. It was non-stop. And what I didn't realise was that the stress of keeping it all going was rising. Trouble with drugs is that you are in the middle of a storm and you don't really know what you are doing.

Once I was in this amusement arcade underneath the flats and we were having some down time, gambling on machines and playing pool and this guy Dickie who was left to run it was a smoker so he was coming to badger us for a bag of weed and in one incident Star wouldn't give him a bag so Dickie hit Star over the head with a big plank of wood. I came round on the scene and heard what happened. We doused him in petrol and I was just about to run round the side and get some matches to set light to him when the police came and everyone ran. And they searched me and found a spliff . They took me down to the station and put me on an identity parade and Dickie said it wasn't me. He was inches away from losing his life cause of my actions. The terrifying thing is I thought nothing of it.

When you are on the streets smoking and drinking you become oblivious to many things. Emotionless. I was going to burn him up and yet he didn't grass me up. That's what it was like in them days. There was a loyalty. The next day we were reading about ourselves in the South London Press, about how some thugs had doused a local man in petrol. Thing was we were laughing about it when we read it. We were laughing a joking about how we got away from it I look back on it now and it seems really serious what we did. He would have died. That's drugs for you. You are caught up in a storm and you can't find your way out of it.

BROADMOOR, 2001

I might go out there on the outside and meet this mysterious woman who nurtures me with love. I try to nurture myself but the pain comes and I go mad. To stop myself from going mad I sing, and write letters. I sometimes talk to a nurse and try and listen to their theories and they say I'm mad. But I say I'm not mad. I just come from a different world from you that's all. It's like they are different people to me. They don't understand it. They are law abiding citizens. They ain't never broken the law. If you ain't broken the fucking law, what is going on? People in power break the law.
When I was in Kings Cross when I was 16 I saw diplomats driving up in their luxury cars with diplomatic number plates buying crack and picking up prostitutes so why are they making a victim out of me. All I want is a slice of the cake. Not being trapped in this hell, no woman. What kinds shit is that? You want a wank they watch you. I been nowhere like this in my life. I can see why so many

took the easy road of suicide but I ain't going to play that part. I must get my rewards. If life was perfect when I was 13, a 45 year old man wouldn't be selling me crack to fuck my head or robbing me in the street to buy a car That person comes back to me to buy crack. It's a vicious circle. Can't take much more of this. I'm going to go through this and come out a winner.

AGED 17 . ROCKS AND DANCES

One time I was in the yard and mixing with the 28s. I was in this .J reg escort — those long ones and I was driving with Dids and my cousin Fitch and feeling cool and good and we went to this rave and there was a big fight going on so I drove past it and decided to pull over and see what was going on. As I stopped to turn off the road I saw there were police behind us who pulled us over "How old are you?" "I'm 30, officer." Thing is I was only 17 but I was driving on my friend's papers so I had to pretend my identity was his. "You don't look 30. Stop fucking us about." "I look young for my age " 33 I told them my name was Gel coz it was my friend's name but they didn't believe me and they made us get out . They didn't discover that we had fifty rocks with us. It was a car full of crack right under their noses. They took us down to Borough police station and they tried to charge me with driving without a license and no insurance. They put me on a three month ban and fined me forty pounds which I paid out of my giro every week it didn't stop me driving. Once you drive you always want wheels. You can't not want to drive so I put on a little cap and glasses so the police wouldn't recognise me.

We soon brought Forty into the car. So we had the car and we'd ride around all day selling the B and the crack and using the money to promote Sovereign dances which we held on Friday nights. We'd live for those nights and spend our money on new outfits to wear to impress the girls. To get the best vibe going we used to import music from Jamaica.

We'd go to Western Union, deposit some of the drug money and send it to Jamaica to some music guys who would cut dubplates which they would send back by express and we would play them at some of the dances we held. We were watching these hip hop artists and thinking that's where all the money was so it was stable and things were going well for Sovereign. Things were good and we were making money. The dream of becoming a big sound. That's what drove me. We was versatile. We'd play hip hop, RnB, jungle, soul.

We like mixed it up in one big pie and that's what was bringing in the people, We had a good following. We started getting more professional. Sollar and some of the other guys even went to Jamaica and met an artist called Bounty killer/hunter who was well known for his dubs. So Sailer would come back with drugs and with dubs he bought off Bounty Killer. Some even went to New York to check out the music scene. When Seller brought the dubs back we used to listen them round me mum's house where there was big stereo and big speakers. We used to have some drugs and cut some dubs of the Bounty Killer sound It was pretty good and we put it on a DAT tape and we played it on the sound system. I don't know why but I never went with them to Jamaica. I was interested in staying and running the fort. There was always more drug deals to do. This was my haven. My mind was trapped as see it now by every day life living in England. I wanted to make enough and stop and become legit but there was so much that happened between that dream and destiny that you never know where you are going to end up. There was this club called Steppers on Coldharbour Lane and we played there with

Sovereign on Wednesday nights and Sundays. It was the only place you got off after a long time on the street and we would be in there drinking champagne and brandy and smoking weed mixed with coke and the girls would be dancing the new style of moves like the Bogle, the Pepperseed, the Butterfly the Tatty, I'd be high and watch girls in middle of dance floor and they would do some X rated dancing, man. Whoa X rated. I'd say "yeah". It was hot and sweaty. But the vibe was good. The Sovereign MCs were our own little stars from Brixton and Streatham and we'd be in competition with the other sound systems to see who could do the best sound. Sometimes we even got some artists over from Jamaica to perform. By now I had a bit of a name for myself and the girls started to sit up and notice. It was a cool vibe and girls would come up to you, a sweet look in their eyes. "Are you a Sovereign man?" "Yeah sweetie I am." "Which one are you?" "I'm Blue." "Aaahh. I've heard all about you." Then they'd get all excited and go off a gossip with their friends. "Rash mate he's flexing." And I'd see them giving me the eye and then they'd come over and they'd be on my dick and they'd be all over me and t was like I'm loving this. I'd be able to take them round to a friend's house and sex them up.

Sometimes my head ached and I'd just be standing at the edge of the dance floor feeling out of it and I'd think, fuck this. I'm going home to bed. 34 Sometimes thought I'd take a girl back to my mum's house. Most of the time my mum never saw but if she did see a girl I brought back she would sometimes give them a stern look. One time my door wasn't locked and the stereo makes an orange light and this girl is sitting on me and mum come in and had a look and then go back in her room. The girl felt pretty discomforted by that "Your mum saw me." °Don't worry about it man.' But you see I did worry about it. I didn't like to cause her upset. I owed a lot to her. Even in them early years we been through some rough times together. And she worried about me coming and going at all times of the day and night. I saw less and less of her. When she did see me she kept nagging me and her voice became heavy and she was moaning the whole time. Sometimes I wouldn't see her for three weeks coz I was staying with friends or at my brother's or sister's. When I did see her and she'd be all on me because she didn't know where I'd been sleeping or what I'd been up to, I'd have to calm her down. "Don't worry about it mum, take it easy. It's cool." Her room was next door to mine and in the morning she would knock on my door. Open up." "I'm tired mum I'm sleeping. Leave me alone." But she'd trick me. "I'm going to work I've left some money on the side." That would usually get me up But when I'd go downstairs she'd be waiting for me. 'What you doing' wid your life. Dee weed is frying' your brain son." One time she sees this gun that I kept in my room. "What's that. It's a gun isn't it?" It was a 38. I told her and she just walked out of the room. She must have known how deep I was in it but she didn't say anything. But sometimes I'd come home and find my shotgun or some knives had gone from the hiding place. I'd look everywhere for them and never find them. She must have hid 'em. I don't know where her hiding place was but it was good. I felt bad for my mum coz the drugs were starting to change my ways.

I should have been saving my money but I weren't. I had a dream once of having my own mobile phone shop, learning some carpentry, owning my own painting and decorating shop, my own business selling gold. The dream never became a reality. My reality was driving in a rental all over London from Dalston in the East to Acton or in West. We'd be flexing, and promoting the Sovereign dances with leaflets about the dances that we'd hand out while we were serving up the gear. Rocks and dances, that's what we were selling. With all the posters and leaflets we sent out we'd get a big turnout. But the thing about it was that the parties never really took off in the way they should. They never became mainstream because people were too afraid to come to the parties because of the guns and we were too blind to see because we were wrapped up in the gun culture.

At the weekends there was always drama and violence at the parties. It was real Yardie time. I'm stressing a little by now coz this is known as the Gunman Sound because in the middle of the tunes there'd be guns blazing away That's what happened when we put it on at dances. Bare gunshots would go off. I was stressing coz I was one of those who perpetrated it. Too much gunshots at dances. It was doing my head in without me realising it. And the business suffered too. Even though business was good there was something wrong coz the money never added up. I'd start off early in the morning, have a spliff of weed and sell off my works during the day. By the time the night comes, I got all my money. Trouble was often I found out I was four hundred pounds short. What's going on? Where's my money gone? It was confusing. But then I realised what was going on. It's all them three pounds and two pounds that were missing. I was spending that on more spliffs more weed and it was eating into my profits. My friends recognised it before I did. 35 You are smoking too much of your own gear. You are going crazy, you are going crazy." But I didn't listen too much. It's hard to trust people in the drug business. I thought they just wanted me out of the game so they could have more punters for themselves. I was getting more and more aggressive with them. I started to get ruthless with these people coz they will walk all over you. I was getting a right turn over. I was getting paranoid with them thinking they were trying to rip me off What I never did realise was that a little seed of paranoia can grow into something very powerful that will take you over. The dealing went on every day but I never got myself out of financial problems. I got a few grand but I was spending as much as I was making. I'd spend a lot on weed, on drinking, on partying. We were partying about three or four times a week.

We'd sometimes park up in the car and just sit and smoke in the car chatting and listening to music, stoned out of our heads. And drug dealing could be a tense business. I had to always be on the lookout. Experience had taught me to be careful and whenever I was walking home I was looking around. Thoughts would always go through me mind if I spied someone too close. Who is that? What's that? What they after? You'd be walking home on the lookout for the feds or for people who were after you. It was a stress. I was paranoid. And sometimes paranoid can be a good thing. But sometimes it can ruin your life And when you get back home, off the streets, it was like, yeah, a relief. I'd eat some Kentucky or a McDonalds, or home cooking like jacket potatoes and steak. I'd be hungry coz of the drugs, it was like there was a monster in my belly. It used to make me weak. Sometimes if I was driving around I'd pull up and go into Kentucky and there'd be a big long queue and I'd push straight to front and everyone gave me a stare. But I didn't care. I couldn't wait. Drugs is numbness to all those niceties. I'd lean over the counter to try and get the food in me as quick as possible. "Two breasts and a classic," It'd be like my energy was leaving me and I couldn't even stand up cos I was so mashed up As soon as the food came I'd eat the chicken and the burger and scoff it down and then I'd have energy again and could stand up. No matter what I ate I couldn't put on no weight. Any food that I had, the drugs ate it all up. But I was never skinny. I was always a big, strong man. I was benching 150 kilos. Guns, drugs, disputes, rivalries. It was chaos.

We all had negativity in our lives and some of the people I was associated with were bringing it on my doorstep. At the time 1 was thinking I had to get involved. And instead of rejecting it, I just gobbled it all up. I was an adrenaline freak. The adrenaline takes you over. It made me become reckless. When it was kicking off, it was like I don't fear nothing, you know what I mean? Like I'm invincible. When I took the crack it was like I can do anything and get away with it. But by the time I realised it was their shit, not mine, it was too late.

BROADMOOR, 2001

What's been happening? I just been sleeping and listening to music and playing snooker. Another day in the life of Mr Blue. I want to go home and get out of this place. I'm going through too much things to explain. It's personal stuff and you can't be telling everyone. I won't say nothing. I don't really want to be talking about what's going on. I've been recuperating some energy. A love affair with the bed? Not a love affair with my bed. I ain't even been going to school. I feel I'm getting the sleep 1 need. 1 need to get out of here and get my life back. My life can only get better. Sometimes I wake up and think, where am I? Then I realize and it's like I'm in a nightmare.

Been in this place almost eight years now. It's time to get out now. Know what I mean? Hit those streets like a bomb and have some fun. Being cooped up is driving me mad, It's like the game up there. All them soldiers and I've been looking at it' and I've seen them at the top of the hill with those swords it's madness. It's hard to be a man when people are fucking with you, poking you, suspecting you, disrespecting you, pushing you in a corner. Of course your head is going to explode and you're going to react or something is going to go wrong. I've been ready to leave since I got here. There are some real aspects that I gotta deal with but I don't know how true they are. It's hard to explain because I can't explain how it works. I gotta learn education and broaden my horizons and improve my vocabulary and learn to talk and speak and the way they tell me to•do this is to bend over. But I don't want to bend over for no man. I don't know how you can have knowledge from someone shagging your arse.

The forces tell me this Mad innit? It's barmy. I got a visit tomorrow from my mum. She's coming up tomorrow for one hour and then visit Russ for an hour. I want to slow down and chill out I get this weird people — its the same. This place is mashing me up something is telling me that I'm the key. The key to what, I don't know. They say it's too soon. My foot's tingling like anything That's the eczema. It's madness. I ain't had this before. This place mashes you up. I've got eczema on my foot and on my hand. I see the doctor yesterday. I told him I want something. But he gave me none. I just want to get out man. I don't see how education works. I understand what is going on now. It was something that came over me. I weren't mad. It's a real thing and it ready happened and I can only look forward now. Rather than keeping on thinking what is going on. I got to move forward. Get out of Broadmoor At the same time, the more I stagger forwards the more I'm in one place.

AGED 18: NEW JACK KIDS

Dids' mum had a friend called Bill who was a Yardie and Dids used to listen to their conversations and he found some good information once. "Do you know Yardie Bill who sells crack? Well he got a flat with bare money in there." He's tight so I got that info and told my friends and one of them knew where he lived so we went round there and broke the door and we found about eight thousand pounds. We took it, went back to our coch and counted out the money and divided it up. I went back there again and found another couple of grand hidden away. So everyone got three or four grand but I must have got eight grand Dids comes up to me. "I wanna invest my money with your money." So we worked out this deal. He bought some crack off me cheap and he would sell it in Kings Cross and give me most of Pie profit So he gave me some money as a deposit and I gave him the crack and off he went.

I was in bed one day and Dids tapped on my window "Blue, give me some more money, man." 'What did you do with the gear I gave you?" "I've sold it all." So I gave him his deposit back. A couple of days later I saw him and he was all crying and desperate. "Blue lend me fifty quid coz I've spent all the money you gave me." "All of it?" "Yeah, all of it." "You gotta give me some more £s." So I gave him some more of the money that he'd given me. The next day I saw him and he was really crying. "Hey Blue, I'm broke again." I worked out that he never even sold the first lot of crack I'd given [him. He'd just gone into a crack house and burned it all down. I still gave him a fifty pound note "Here. Take this. Don't come to me no more. I don't want to know." They suspected it was us. This guy called Chism, who worked in a shop, selling a lot of coke over the counter and was an associate of Yardie Bill he said 'You robbing my base. Watch what happens to you." So we thought they might be working science on us some sort of black magic. Everyone that robbed that house, misfortune took them. Sadda was doing well, then his money ran out and he coked out. Star's money ran out and he coked out and Dids' money ran out and he coked out. And that left me. I was the only one doing well. And look at my downfall. Sadda was juggling in Kings Cross and he was doing well flexing and the next minute he flopped he was working for my cousin Titch and Titch was working for Dandy and then Star was flexing and he bought a little motor and he was flexing bad, his money flopped and he was smoking and they all came to me. "I know I owe you Blue but I ain't got no money. Take this as payment." They all said the same thing. "I owe you Blue." "Lend us fifty quid Blue." "Take this as payment, Blue." What they all started doing was paying me with crack. And instead of selling it I was burning it down. So now I'm fucked up on crack. I needed to collect some of my debts.

One time I saw Cheeks, the guy who used to feed the younger ones crack to get them hooked. He was walking up Brixton High Street. He owed me £100 for some crack I'd given him "Where's my money?" He kept on making excuses. Bang, so I thumped him. He dropped to the floor. 'Where's my money?" He got up and jumped over the bollards on Brixton Road and I chased him all the way to his house. "Give me my money." "I haven't got it. I haven't got it." So I go and get me gun and go back to his house. This time his mum comes to the door and gives me half the money. I never got the rest. But the hunger didn't stop.

We were at the Cross and we were there with a shotgun a 22 and a 25 in the car and we would see someone with chops or gold chain and jack the car and stick it up. We'd be robbing people and going around with guns in the car. It was utter madness. It was a proper new jack business. I was controlled by the crack. I was sucking it but this time I was popping it, I was properly smoking it and it was making me crazy. I'd be in Kings Cross with a gun in my waist, looking fly in all the latest but I was losing my judgement and so were all my friends. Out there in Kings Cross spitting out stones, fighting with other dealers, fighting with police and it was pure madness. Why don't I have a normal nice business this is madness. It was getting too hectic for me. Fuck this. If I get caught I'm going to go to jail. It was my beef with Little L that set off a whole sequence of bad events. It all started over a jacket, an expensive jacket that I'd bought with my earnings. It was a really good long leather jacket that cost me £500. Little L was this guy t knew from Peckham who knew my cousin Titch I invested in some gear with Titch my cousin and then we started dealing with the Peckham boys and everytime I went to get my money they gave us big rocks to smoke and I started smoking it and really feeling the effects and I was thinking they are taking the piss. They were buying £1000 pounds jackets and anyway I got some shit and sold it. Things were getting out of control.

One time Titch, Dids, Little L were in some girls flat in Kings Cross and they were smoking and they fell asleep and Dids stole their cash and their drugs and they found him a few days later walking in Kings Cross. They shot him twice in the back and went up to him and beat him in the face with the gun, pistol whipped him till the gun was bent up. The ting was they were all happy about the beating they gave him. Especially Little L. "I gave him a Goodfellas. I gave him a real Goodfellas." Coz in this flat in Kings Cross we used to watch all these gangster movies — King of New York, Scarface, Mobsters. We were all acting out characters out of the film. Dids was laid up in hospital after the shooting and that's when the police caught him and he was sent down for his crimes, cases that were outstanding. It wasn't till

Dids came out that Little L. Titch and Dids made it up. Dids robbed this shotgun and gave it to Titch and Little L to smooth things out as a way of saying sorry.

In the meantime I'd lent Little L my leather jacket. And that's where it started to go wrong. Titch and Little L were doing something with the shotgun. They sticked up someone or something like that and drove to this girl's house in Wood Green and the police were following them and they chased them and threw the gun in the garden and ran through the bushes and Titch got arrested for firearms. Little L got away but as he was escaping he lost my jacket in the commotion. So winter came and that s how I got into a beef with Little L I was with Star when we confronted him. "Give me my jacket back. I told you not to wear it." He wouldn't give it back to me "Well give me some money then as payment " "Hey man I'll give you back some money later." "I want it now Give me your chops then." Chops means bracelet His was a 3 ounce gold bracelet He wouldn't do it. "You just have to wait a bit. I'll get your money for you." Something in me just clicked and I !limped him in his mouth and bear hugged him. I really scrunched him His teeth flew out and rocks wrapped in clingfilm flew out and Star started picking up the rocks and took off his bracelet and gave the rocks back to him. "Star, what the fuck are you doing? Take the chops and rocks off him." So Star takes the bracelet away and I threw him on the floor, took his bracelet and put my face right in his. "See that's how you get robbed pussy." So anyway, I started walking back and he gets up and has a go at me. 'No man, that's not haw it works. I don't get stabbed and I don't get shot.' I didn't want to take no back chat from him. "You wanna die like a hero man, fuck off. Now you do it my way, you come down the estate and you give me money and I'll give you back your chops." All jump back in the car ready to drive off but the guy is hung on to the trimmings and he was shouting as we tried to drive away. "No one ain't robbing me like that. I don't get shot or stabbed. You won't get away with robbing me." I shouted back at him. "Hang on like that and you are going to die like a hero." Anyway, we didn't want to drive away with him hanging on the car and the police coming over. Because we had a gun in the car and all. So we stopped the car. That's when he relented. "I'll get you your money."

"Alright, meet us down in the estate." So we drove off down the estate and waited for him underneath the garages. But while we were waiting word came to me that he'd went down Peckham to get a 38. Rellie told me. But I knew they wouldn't give nothing to Stockwell boys coz they didn't trust us. So we got the Luger out and worked out a plan with Star. Wait for him to give me the cash When he asks for his chops, you draw the gun and tell him he ain't getting no chops coz we already give it back to him." When Lithe L arrived he spoke first. "Give me the chops." "You do it by my rules. Give me the money first." So he gave me the money. Then he puts his hand out for the drugs,- e, "OK. Now you give me the chops." But that was never our plan and Star draws the Luger on him. "Fuck off Star or I'll shoot you." And he gets all worked up. "Go on then shoot me. Yeah shoot me." So I turn to Star 'Don't shoot him coz he wants to die like a hero." Anyway, we turned to go and he won't leave us. He follows us all the way back to Star's house. That's when I flipped. I pushed the gun up in the guy's face. Star gave him a rap. "Move away from my fucking house or we'll shoot you." That seemed to do it. Little L went off and bought some crack off Forty and disappeared from the estate. But it weren't the end of the story. A couple of days later I get a phone call from one of Little L's friends. It was a challenge. "Come to Peckham if you think you're bad." It was a declaration of war Me, Titch, Forty. Star. Illie and me against Little L and his crew.

We rose to the challenge We were a big group of guys going to work, soldiers in the war between Peckham and Brixton.

We come to this place in Peckham and all we had was one bullet in the Luger and so we also took the 22 with one bullet. So we only got two shots. We get to this address and there's a party going on and that's when we see them all lined up in a room and this one man Vin Park is there. "Come on man, I need to talk to you outside. You man shouldn't be warring." So me and Titch go outside but it was a bait. As we got outside now, the Peckham boys must have drawn a gun coz all I see is Star running down the street with Little L chasing him. So my cousin Titch takes off down the road with the 22 and chases Little L. I shout after them don't run, stand up to him." But they don't listen to me they just carry on running turned to Vin Park "You set me up to draw a gun but I will deal with you later." Then I see Forty turning the car round and I jump into the car and we drive down to where Little L. Titch and Star are involved in a confrontation. And as Little L goes to shoot Star the gun jams on him, so I get involved and Little L jumps up and tries to head-butt me so I get my knife out and stab him in his face and then others from the Peckham crew get involved and suddenly there is a bang and I feel this deep pain in my leg By this time everyone has run away because of the gunshot. So I try and run too and I stagger to this petrol station and I see my leg is bleeding. That's when I realise that I been shot. So I stop this guy next to the petrol pump "Hi give you a tenner if you drop me off at home." "What happened?" "Someone shoot me in the leg." So he drop me home on the estate and I phone my friends. 'Where are you?" We crashed the car. Were walking back to the estate: It turns out Forty crashed the car in Denmark Hill as they were making a getaway. By the time they get back my leg was bleeding badly so they give me some crack to numb the pain "I know a hospital were you won't get into trouble. I got family down there." I rubbed some coke on the wound and got in a cab and went to hospital. I limped into the hospital and began to tell some porkies "I got some metal in my leg. I cut myself on a metal railing.' They X rayed it and found there was no bullet or nothing there so they bandaged me up and sent me on my way without asking too many questions.

So I got back on the estate and all this was going on when we were meant to be making money so from then on I said I'm not walking nowhere So we talked about what happened and it turns out that they shot Little L in the mouth but the bullet hit him in a tooth and came out. No one seemed to know who had shot me in the leg coz they shot me discreetly, But it didn't end there. A few weeks later the feud was still going on. Me and Titch had bought this 32 gun from Sonnet and he used to keep it above a cab office in Earls Court and someone stole it. And anyway I was in my house on a Sunday and I'd just had a bath and Illie and Titch came round. "Come on over to Steppers coz I got the ting on me so everything's OK." "Give me the gun." "No I'll hold onto it." I thought fuck it. Maybe it's best if they keep it. Some brown skinned guy with an afro who owned a cab took us there. When I got out at Steppers there was a whole line of Peckham boys there. They knew I was going to be there coz I was regular. I knew they were there to get me. So I jump out of the cab and slip into the back of the club and see Forty. "You got your ting on you?" "Yeah I got my Luger." "Give me your gun." So by the time I'm getting the luger and coming back to the dance floor and I've now put it in me waist and we were at the back and some guy called Smoky is there and he says "Yeah, Little L's out there and he wants his chops back off you. He wants to talk to your cousin." I'm thinking fuck, what's he on their side for? And so I went out there and I was talking to Titch. What kind of message is that?" And he says, "Listen man, I ain't sayin nuttin" So I went outside and most of my friends were there, my older friends and all the Peckham guys were there and so I'm talking to Little L can I have my ting's back. "I got nothing for you 'star" And I look down and he's got a 9mm Koch and I thought raah he means business. He wanted to get me. So I grabbed it from his pocket and we were grappling with it and my cousin is shooting and shooting and all I'm seeing is sparks going all over the place and while we were fighting for the gun there was a Peckham guy pushing me so I grabbed it and he got his gun out and was waving it around firing and I look around and there's all the Brixton crew watching me fight this Peckham man and they're shouting "fuck you." And now my cousin Titch is shooting and I'm thinking who's he shooting at? And the rest of my crew just seem to be standing there watching me. Now come no one ain't helping me? Anyway, I pushed Little L into the gutter and run through the Peckham mandem, ran into a corner and the gun dropped to me ankle, so I pick it up and I came out running towards Steppers firing. And it wouldn't fire. All I hear is, "run, run, run." Everyone is scattering and I'm trying to fire the gun but it's not firing and was thinking what's wrong with this, maybe there are no bullets? So I ran out squeezing the trigger but it still wouldn't fire so I put it back to safety and cocked the thing and ran out again and it still wouldn't fire so I pulled out the magazine and tried it again and it still didn't fire. Then I hear the police sirens and I run through all bare backstreets and got back into Stockwell Park estate and phoned the guys. 42 "What kind of gun you give me? It won't fire." "It weren't cocked properly." I didn't know whether they were having me on so I cocked it and tested it on the estate. "Bang, bang, bang." It fired pretty well. They were right, it wasn't cocked properly. They apologised for not telling me how it worked. All the old guys came up to me and started bigging me up and showing me respect. 'Well done man, you done well. Respect." "Well done man you made a good escape." They were congratulating me on the whole situation. After this day I wondered about it and I thought that maybe they were trying to assassinate me. I thought maybe it was a plot against me, coz my cousin is firing and there were sparks coming out. I thought there were no one on my side. I was fighting a man with my gun and no one was helping me. Why were they just watching me? Maybe they just wanted me to get killed. It pissed me off. I had questions going round me head. How come Peckham man come down here and no one don't protect me? The Yardie man gave them guns. I had to protect myself so that I wasn't in vulnerable situation. Those were the paranoid thoughts going around me head. It was the drugs making me paranoid. Sometimes though it is healthy paranoia. It's survival isn't it. But those thoughts can also drive you crazy It was the next day we discovered that a ten year old girl had been shot in the crossfire and the Peckham guys were blaming us for shooting but it weren't us but it was him that let it off while I was fighting with him for the gun. But the family were blaming my cousin and in the end my older brother said he would come with us to get the guys. But no one wanted to defend the argument, so I thought they were wankers man. There was a big outcry coz of the shooting of the girl. So the police did all these house searches looking for Yardie gunmen. It didn't end there We wanted revenge. One night we were all tooled up in this dead end bit of the Stockwell Park estate — a 22, the Luger, a 32 and a shotgun and we were going to go to Peckham and hit on them and this guy called Butler and he said "If you got anything on you I think you should get rid of it because the police is coming." Lucky he said that because we turned this corner and the police were everywhere. Everyone ran in their own direction. I ran for my life and got to the other part of the estate and hid the gun. We all got away but Forty he nearly got trapped and he tried to run upstairs and he put the gun through some girl's letter box but it wouldn't go through. He tried to put it in the electricity meter cupboard but it wouldn't go so in the end he knocked on someone's door and this old woman answered and he gave her twenty pounds just to pretend to talk to him so that when the police arrived he looked all innocent.

We were sure that someone had tipped off the police but we never found out who. In the end the police raided Star's house and found bullets in his trainers. He got arrested and sent to jail for possessing those bullets. Before he went to jail he gave me his mobile phone. "Look after business for me while I'm gone." So I took the business over he had bare punters and I was making two thousand pounds a day. I was getting close to where I wanted to be — the biggest tiger in the jungle.

BROADMOOR, 2001

That war it's still going on. I'm not going back to that war anymore. Life has gone on.
Seven years down the line. I got scores to settle. Scores with my homeboys who betrayed me. I'm going to play it cool. I'm not going for war. It's a dog eat dog game. 43 What got me back here is me turning into a dog, I keep on turning into this dog. The doctors want my arse. The staff want my arse. They want to give me blow jobs. Someone tells me this and my head goes into space and all kind of stuff happens. Why do I get into this? Someone is playing tricks with me with evil spells trying to make my life fucked up while I'm in here so I can't come out. I got to get a plan to deal with this. I got to get a plan to deal with this. I can't relay my ideas. When you are dealing with these things you gotta keep them to yourself or it won't work, NI be able to sort him out. There's more powerful people than him. That's the main thing. If

it was true and could get out it would be good. This is another episode of this they change my medication. I feel a bit drugged up. I'm on Solpret. It made me feel drowsy and bad I'm telling myself if this is true I want to get out of here. I think someone is playing tricks on me. I used to run with dogs so I turned into a dog. Whoever you run with you become like. It's maybe what you want. You keep coming back to it, too powerful. If I don't follow it, it's telling me the sun won't shine, I'm not going home, I won't meet my friends, I won't get my own life back. I think this must be madness. I know myself well enough to know that anything I do is something that will benefit me. They are powerful ideas. That's what I'm saying. It's like a force. Someone's cursed me. They are playing tricks with me. Since I ain't been getting my mum's cooking it's been going on. And from that guy that visited me. That demon who brought me to see that man. Whatever they are trying to do they are trying to fuck me up. But everything comes to those who wait and everything happens for a reason. Everything you do in life has its adverse effect. I kill people one day I might get killed. I'm in here, they are out there. Whatever they are doing to me, whatever is going on out there, they'll get killed or they'll get locked up. It's a vicious circle. So I can sort my head out and get the fuck out of here. Being on an even keel. That's what I want. No nonsense in my head, at peace with myself and then I can make my move. These doctors are meant to do that I feel better on this pill they gave me. I feel more chilled out, enough to get ready to do whatever I have to do. I depend on the pills for the meantime The family's got something to do with it. Everything will come to pass. I don't read my bible anymore. That's why I feel things might get a bit funny. I read it and I'm still in here so I leave the book alone And keep out of trouble to survive in this hellish habitat. Outside is hell and outside is heaven. And when 1 get out I intend to make my life go to heaven. I was coming to see Jule on this ward and I came up and said when em you going to see me? Maybe I speak too much of my mind. I'm looking for help. Chill out is the first half step. I'm just taking time out I've got to get my life together. Seven years I've been like this. It's gonna rain, you gotta get ready, you better get right. God is coming. You'll see the light. It's going to rain, I'm telling you It's like i died and came back. I'm told I'm schizophrenic, told say to them, it's funny, I buy a new Snoop Dog album, it's called the last meal, he's in a cell behind the bars and there's a screw bringing rice and chicken. Are you taking the piss? Snoop's free. What's he doing in a picture like that. It's the last meal. I don't get no more food. There are a lot of coincidences and I'm wondering and trying to work it out. Where's the realistic side of it and I'm none the wiser. Hoggy dog, doggy, snoop dog. So what is it all about? I do enjoy these therapy sessions. It's a privilege. Something dark is fucking with me. I dunno find a way out of it. You know what dispels dark? Light dispels dark. Something tells me I'm the sun. The sun doesn't shine. I can make you look at the sun. The sun, why is it doing this to me but they say I'm ill and they keep me here in Broadmoor. I'm not perfect, nobody's perfect. They tell me I'm wrong and mad and all I try and do is get help.

AGED 18: CRACK KING

My crack business was going well. I got a good name for myself. I had the reputation as selling the biggest stones in the area. Old times players were bringing me in the game and if there was any beef with any of the punters they would try and squash it for me. I had a few yardies who I was buying my gear from. One of them was a DJ, another a bouncer. Sometimes there was a drought when no crack was coming onto the estate and the price goes up but most of time I had a good rapport with my suppliers. To start off with I got drugs on consignment and paid back afterwards, but later I was buying my own supply. Nobody gave me fuck all. I paid my own way. I'd pay £1,250 for an ounce of crack and I'd sell it for £2,500. Double my money. To cut the competition I made sure I got the biggest stones. For a time I was the A list dealer in Stockwell. My phone rang the whole time from eight in the morning till three the next morning. It was a 24/7 business. People would be all over me. "Blue, Blue, sell me some shit. Please Blue." "Blue, Blue pay you back tomorrow," "Blue, I'll be here tomorrow with the money." I was getting a reputation for being the best. Sometimes people would be banging on my window chasing down the shit. "Blue, I just robbed a jewellery shop. Take this and give me some rocks." They'd give me the jewellery that they'd stolen and I'd look at it and give them some money. Then I'd sell it on. Business was good. I paid a hundred pounds for a brand new, white gold Omega woman's watch and sold it on for seven hundred pounds. I was an entrepreneur. I never worked out what I was making on a weekly basis. A few grand but I spent it on cars, gold, clothes, looking after people. See, I had these hangers on, that were skimming the cream. I was buying things with assets. I didn't really know how to handle the money. I was buying cocaine and champagne, the high life, and getting accustomed to it I started mixing with guys who were driving Mercs and Porsches. They'd turn up in their luxury cars, park near the estate and I would sell them a few rocks. In them days it seemed like the crack business was like a democracy. Crack was the drug of pauper and king alike. But it got to the point when I started wondering about all these well-dressed guys coming onto the estate Why are they all buying off me? It took me a few weeks before I realised they were not smoking my shit. What I hadn't realised was that they were buying my shit and selling it on. They had their own franchises and they were getting rich on it. And the key to their success was that they don't get high on their own supply. But I didn't know it at the time. What I used to do was burn a bit with them and talk with them. They were always into the talk. "Blue, you are the man. We come to you coz you are honest. You treat us good not like some of the others on the road." They would say such and such is a pussy or so and so is fucked up. They were always playing me off with another one. They were always dissing each other And it got to the point when I asked myself. Why are they always talking about each other? Why are they slagging everyone off? Why is there no harmony? When you are dealing crack the whole time it's a difficult business. You have to keep your supply lines open. You have to get the punters in, you have to manage the money. You have to watch your back. And anxiety creeps up on you slowly became wary of those man. I thought they are trying to turn me stupid Be careful Blue. I had to protect myself. So all their talk I was absorbing it but not watching it. I was always smiling. The smile was a crooked smile. One day I'm gonna be the man. That's what kept me going. But you know what? It's stressful watching your back It's stressful when there's no unity. And I was in the middle of it. Don't get me wrong. I played the game too. I slagged off some of the others. But I stayed loyal to one player, Little Dandy, He had my back, I didn't say anything about him to anyone. Something was holding me to him Me and his brothers used to hang around. We hung around in the hood together. And now he's dead. But that was my aim. To be a big player in the game. To be the man. And that's when it started to go wrong by now I've started mixing with the 28s and I got Blood to work for me and he always came up to me and called me up, always demanding more and more. He was a good worker, always serving for me. "I'm out of gear. I'm out of gear." So I drove down there and loaded him up and loaded him up with working . This was before me and Sollar went our own way, must have got up about '10 grand.

BROADMOOR 2001

I'm on injections and Temazepam to help me chill out. It's doing the job. It's keeping me well. I want to get motivated, rapping and moving and not sitting on my arse. Christmas is coming and it's doing my head in. You should be with the family at Christmas. If they let me out tomorrow I wouldn't be the same player that I used to be. I would be the one sitting at home receiving the money not out on the street running around. That ain't my scene no more. I done that. I will have to eliminate the competition. I've been suffering for years. I don't want the headache of not knowing where the next bit of cash is coming from. I want to see my nieces and nephews. And my son. Some people

.say I got a son. They say he's just like me. He's a little me.

AGED 18 (contd): TIME OUT

For a short while there was some sense in me. The life I was leading was too crazy. I knew I had to get out. So I went back down to the estate and chilled out and sweated out the drugs. I stayed in and my mum was rubbing me in oil and bathing me. She knew something was wrong. She started feeding me and giving me ginseng to eat and I got fit and instead of smoking every day I smoked only on the weekend and made some money throughout the week from some small deals. I was juggling on the estate again but this time I wasn't smoking the profit or spending it on the high life. I was making enough just to feed myself, keep healthy and go back on the market. But it was too much for me. My mum tried to get me into doing carpentry and to tell the truth I did think about it but the lure of the streets was too big. You sit down in your house and you look around and you think that my mum has toiled all her life and she's spent all her money on her kids and she's not driving, she's renting a house in a rough area. These are the thoughts that cross your mind. Man. I don't want this. This is bullshit. Go and work for the man and have nothing and pay taxes and council tax and poll tax. If I'm gonna work I want a job that is going to give me some proper amount of money but it always comes back to education and I ain't got no education. I had tried to get an apprenticeship so I can learn the craft, working and doing theory and when I tried it they closed the door on me. It was hard in those times. Young black men weren't getting jobs. It was better to be on YTS or giro and smoking on the streets. And when crack came along you think I can get some power here and make something for myself. I am going to take a chance. And when you start rolling into this lifestyle you see the power and influence you have over people and it's like a status and you come to enjoy it and the more you enjoy it the more it gets you and the more powerful your mind starts to develop and more corrupt and even more evil. And I missed having the money and life started to become hard again, a real struggle. I needed to get back in the game. All along my mum was saying there ain't no such thing as a friend. She used to tell me, All the people you see as friends, just you see. You see what happens to them when you are in trouble. You see what happens when they let you down," I was thinking that my mum was just jealous and that she didn't like me being with my friends. There was a lot of confusion in my mind. I was thinking that's just my mum. She doesn't understand. She'll see one day what a team me and my mates make and we'll be millionaires And while there was loyalty to my mum, there was loyalty to my homies. It was a delicate balance. Your homies are trying to get you out on the streets and your desires and dreams and ambitions for a moral life become cross faded coz you are with friends who would die for you and you say to yourself I've got to deal with them like a family as well because this is the brotherhood because if they've got a problem or need money you have got to provide for them as well. Do good unto them because they do good unto you. I made the decision to hit the streets again. A friend helped me out and gave me a couple of quarter bags. I cashed the giro and got sixty quid for that. I bought a 1/6 of an ounce of brown. That made ten bags which I sold for a £100. With that one hundred quid I bought an eighth, I sold that I bought a quarter with the proceeds. Sold that. Then I bought an ounce and sold it. Then I had money to play with. I didn't spend any money on myself and I stayed off the crack. I was back in business. I turned the money from the heroin to buy a 16 th of crack, then an 8 th , then a quarter then a half ounce crack, Yep, I was back in the crack business. This time though I kept it to myself. I kept my friends out of it. They ain't no good. They didn't help me when I was down. I carved up a little corner of London which I kept for myself. It was Turnmills nightclub in Farringdon. That's where I met my customers. I didn't realise to start with that it was a gay club but it didn't matter. I was back in business. By now I'd saved up about £5,000, so I bought myself a nice set of wheels. I didn't want nuthin' that will bring the law on me. I looked in the auto pages and found this convertible Escort for £3,000 and a D registration convertible Volkswagen Golf for £2.000. I decided on the Golf. I rang them and said I'm coming over. It was in Hampstead Heath and there were all these big houses with gates and cameras. Wow, I thought. This is the place to live man. This will be the ultimate dream. In the end it was a B reg but it was clean and nice so I bought it. As we got back down south it started playing up. The next day when I went to start it, would the car drive? I says to myself, What is wrong with this car? This is a mash-up. So, I called the people and went back there to get my money back but there was no one there. I went to a Volkswagen garage and they said it was £1,500 to fix it. Fucking hell. I just spent two grand on it and what a waste of money. In the end a friend fixed it up for £800 but it never really worked that well. It was a good lesson.

There are scam artists even in the most poshest areas. But now I've got wheels and feel better and I think I can mix with my friends again. So they start coming round again and sure enough I'm fully back in the game. Forty's brother got hold of some good shit that was cheap so we sold that and soon they were all wanting convertibles. It wasn't long before everyone had followed my lead and the whole estate was full of convertibles. There was a Peugeot, a red Escort, Sollar had a Golf, Forty too. We were back living the high life, driving around in Versace with the roof off and going to clubs and parks and we had tools hidden in the car just in case. I had so much work going on that I employed three workers, Miniman, Beaver and Stripes. They did all the making money for me while I was driving around doing nothing, playing out in clubs in London and Nottingham and Birmingham and we were just enjoying life. I just gave my workers the supply and collected the money and stayed out of harm's way. I was beginning to see my dream come true. I was getting to where I wanted to be. The Big Man on the road. The only thing that went wrong was that someone on the estate was out for revenge for something. And to this day I don't know what I'd done wrong. They poured sugar in my petrol tank. Life was good again. But the arguments and disagreements and drama never totally went away. And they were ready to go up a level.

BROADMOOR, 2001

I don't know d I get enough compassion from doctors and people in high up positions like police and judges. My offenses occurred when my mind wasn't right. My actions were taken in a way when it wasn't in the realistic world. I did go for help. Negligence from team before I was even seen. I tried to prevent what happened, but it happened and it was cry for help. But they are making an example of me. Why make a victim out of me? They're taping my phone calls. They monitor my visits. A witness got killed in my case. They might think I want to gun someone down. They think I got all these Gs on my visit list. The truth is only one of them comes and sees me. But he's left the Gangster life behind. He's into family life. He's no player. He's trying to survive and make his family eat. Bring me a trainer I phone my brother, my sister and my girlfriend. I'm trying the best I can, My mind is going round m circles. I'm trying hard. But no one will give me a chance. I just need to be given that chance. Just being back with your family can make a man's heart so full of joy you can change altogether. Seven years of lonely nights. Its terrible In seven years I ain't done nothing that serious deal with my feelings in a ghetto way. First time I cried in 3 or 4 years was recently. I realised how fucked up I had been so far and what changes I can do. You have to play the cards that you've been given. I ain't getting much access at the moment. Something will pop up. I've had two aces — the music and just being alive. To tell the story. 1 feel inferior in places like this. I just hope someone wants to hear my story. I think they will I'm locked down but I'm not giving up the fight.

AGED 18 (cont'd) : SNOOP

The music we were into was now rap. 1 loved all those rap artists. Tupac and Snoop. They rapped about my life and they were making money from it. So when I got word that Snoop Dog was coming to Brixton I was excited. I was on the corner with about twenty friends when Larder and Little Dandy and a couple of other men came up. They wanted some money. If not they were going to distress the Snoop show and take it over and some crap. They were going to mash up the job. There were these guys with an outfit called Rampage at Red records who were organising the show and Little Dandy was ready to extort them. "Give us 20 grand or we'll distress the show so that it won't go on." The Rampage boys were clever and instead of paying up they took us for a night out at Equinox nightclub to charm us. We went straight through into the club without having to speak to the doormen. It was a good night. I spent most of the time watching the girls dancing. We then got invites to the show and people got paid off and they gave Little Dandy contacts so he could bring Snoop over on his own account. The first show went off alright, so Little Dandy set about organising a Snoop show 'We want £20,000 investment per person and we reckon you will get 25% back if it's a success. - I did think about it but I had my own plans. I had my Golf convertible to maintain and was looking to invest in a new set of wheels. I had an expensive lifestyle. Every new gig required a new outfit. The old gear becomes casual clothes after a white. I had drugs to buy and reinvest in, I had hangers on who I had to look after. I tried to give my mum some money although I never gave her as much as I should have. So, I never had much loose change. I decided not to invest in the show. But Little Dandy was on a mission. He was going to get money for that show whatever happened And the worst thing did happen There were this fisherman's shop in Brixton run by Mr Spliffington. Little Dandy and Larder went round there looking for money for the Snoop concert. 'We need 20 gs from you to invest money in the show. What can you give us?" "Come back on Thursday and I'll see what I have." So my cousin Titch, Finger, Larder, Dannay and Dandy went round there on Thursday but this time the bloke's reaction was a bit different. "No, I can't get the money." That got Finger, Larder and Little Dandy got upset. So they boxed this tray of West Indian patties to the floor and started threatening the owner. It was getting a bit hectic and there was this Dread there called Dannay. And Spliffer went into the back of the shop and came out with a 45 and started firing shots. Dandy and Dannay ran out of the shop with Spliffer pointing the 45 at his back and firing at him as he ran down the road. Four bullets hit Little Dandy in the back. Luckily an ambulance was driving past as he collapsed on the pavement. They picked him up and rushed him straight to Kings College hospital. The older heads were smiling and laughing about it. I think they thought he'd got what he deserved. I got in the car and drove straight down the hospital where there was already a group of friends and relatives crying outside the emergency area and nurses and doctors were running about. It was pretty chaotic. "Is he going to make it?" 'We don't know." Bullets had peppered his back. No one knew how far they'd penetrated. One of his relatives was there. "He wants to see you." They showed me in and there was a few of the other guys there and from then on we took it in turns sitting at his bedside and watching him to make sure that no one tampered with the controls. He had a few beefs with people so no one was sure if someone would try and finish him off. And of course he knew who shot him. 48 It was round this time that Titch, my cousin had introduced me to a girl called Tasha. She was from Stoke Newington but she used to come to the hospital with me. That whole time was a vulnerable time for me. It ain't good seeing your friend all mashed up in hospital with tubes coming out of his mouth and nose. My friend got shot. It hurt me. The head of things got shot That's when I thought about my life and I just wanted to change. This is not right. If he can get shot anyone of us can get shot. I realised I needed to get a job and settle down. All I'm saying about everything is that there was this moment when I realised it was wrong and I wanted to adjust my life and settle down and get a girl have a few kids and get a job. Stop smoking drugs and drinking That's all I wanted. It was a wake-up call. I was kinda looking at the game in a different perspective after that. The main man had been shot He'd nearly died so we all looked at life in a different way. It really shook me up. It shook me still. I'm not denying it It shook me You see, the thing was, Dandy, the main man had once taken me aside to talk to me. "Once inside this life, you never get out." Now I knew what he meant. For the first time in my life I started opening up to someone. There was something about Tasha that made me want to confide in her She was pretty. She was level-headed. I'd go and visit her after visiting Dandy in the hospital. I was worried. The things I were doing, the guns and shootouts and it can happen to anyone, anyone can get taken out of the game. So reality started sinking in. "You know what? This life ain't for me man. This life ain't for me." She started talking to me, reassuring me, getting me to open up about my life. It was like experiencing a lot of things to each other. I revealed a lot of secrets to her. I was vulnerable I guess I felt lonely. I showed her my whole game. I opened it all up to her. She understood coz she was a street girl from another manor. She knew how it worked. She understood. The thing what was good was Tasha. I began to think differently about girls. It was like raah this girl is constructive. I started feeling for her. I showed her the corners where we used to deal back in the day. I showed her where we used to hold parties. I told her that this is where the shit happens. It was like showing her my castle. She was a shoulder to lean on. I was in shock. I needed someone to talk to and a woman's shoulder is a nice place to lean on. I didn't know much about her. She was a nice girl and I was getting acquainted with her. I wanted to get out of the game. I wasn't Stared. It was like a message I can go any time. I suddenly realised I'm not invincible. I asked myself questions. Is it worth all this? I revealed all my bad secrets. She took it well. She loved it. She was giving me advice. "Something is going to happen to you one day unless you listen to me." "Naa. Nothing won't happen to me." "Listen Matty. All these girls you go around with, it's not good for you. You mix with the wrong people "It's nothing. Things will be alright." I was blind to what was coming. Dandy was weeks in hospital. But he discharged himself. He didn't want to miss the Snoop concert. When the day of the Snoop concert finally came round, we were all excited. I took Tasha with me. She was looking pretty hot Perhaps too hot. She was wearing this woollen dress that revealed everything. "You too ashamed to walk with me?" She meant it as a joke but it is hard walking around with a girl when every man's eyes are trained on her. Anyway, we went to the front of the show and had a blast. There was this strange moment for me when Dr Dre was rapping to the audience "When you smoke weed your heart goes boom, boom, boom, boom." I got this strange sensation. And I felt my heart beating boom, boom, boom, boom. Dr Dre was continuing his rap. When you smoke cocaine it goes bom bom, bom bom, bom bom." And my heart did that, I felt like it was a spiritual connection with the music. It was affecting me, I've remembered that moment ever since. It was either something profound that I felt, or the beginnings of my illness, or both. Afterwards I went backstage and was chilling with my home boy and he flipped. Dandy was there in a wheelchair. Next day there was another Snoop show and I went this time with the 28s. At the time the Stockwell man dem were shining and the 28s were old school. But I didn't see it like that. I tried to bring the two groups together. I'd told some of the Stockwell boys that we could join up. "He should bring them in and we can eat food together." It didn't go well. There were some in Stockwell who would never get along with the 28s. It was that rivalry that caused the skuffle. This Stockwell man called Puplet was on the door of the Snoop concert that night and I went over to talk to him. And he says your crew are inside." What he was saying was that he was surprised to see me with the 28s rather than hanging out with the Stockwell crew. For me there was nothing wrong. And I told him so- I'm here with this lot tonight." Suddenly, out the blue, this bouncer comes from nowhere, punches me and lands me on the railings. I'm laying on the railings and I was getting thumped up, Some stupid mad punter has hit me in my face. That was my first thought. I come to my senses and I think fuck this. And I grabbed his legs and picked him up and run to wall with him and threw him and I punched him. There was a bare fight going on until the police arrived. The police were asking me my name and address and I gave a bogus name and I had thirty rocks on me but they didn't search me which was pretty lucky. I went home and was going to get my gun to blaze him down, but there were too many police around so I went to get a knife and some CS gas, which a friend had smuggled in from France. I put on a bandanna and a baseball cap and got on my mountain bike and I stood on the corner with the 28s chilling and smoking weed, waiting for my moment. "I'm gonna fuck that guy up." Someone said the man, Rellie, a Stockwell man, has gone down the road. I rid down there so fast on my bike I was going to lunge him up. But he got away. I was a bit forward. I think they were playing me. I never did really learn why that man came at me. There was a girl at the show who I'd upset and maybe he was out to get revenge for her. Or they were taking revenge for not investing in the show. Or they didn't like me hanging out with the 28s. I thought there was enough food for everyone to eat but some in Stockwell or from the Untouchables didn't want the 28s on their turf muscling in on their drug deals. Who knows why I was hit. The truth is though that these guys change like the weather. Maybe Tasha could have pulled me out of that life. See I was attached to her spiritually and mentally. But I just couldn't stay true to her. It was the dog in me. I can see a nice girl and I want to get to know her even though I've got one at home A dog is a beast he just wants more girls. All of my generation were going through the same thing — notches under the belt. We'd be boasting to each other. "I had six girls this week." "Yeah well I had two in a day." That standard was there from day one in that life. You must understand what I'm saying right? It's not only us that behaved like dogs. I read books and even posh writers talk about the same kind of things. Loads of men have the same experiences in their childhood finding it hard to settle down and it wasn't only the men's fault. The girls were coming for it too. If you had money, a nice car and clothes, the girls were attracted. They are looking for a man who can support them. Sometimes they think that a player will do that. Either you would be faithful with them or you tell them it's open, or you move on. You don't even have the time to get to know the girl in that life. She looks good and you want to get to know her and have sex with her. The ultimate goal is to get rich and establish yourself. The object of being a player in the game is to make as much money as you can, become legit and have the basic necessities that the world has to offer -a car, house, a woman, but you want it in three years, not ten years. But in those three years so much shit can happen that the dream can become a hell. The gun battles, the knife fights, the drug selling, the parties and girls and you can get side tracked and being in here has opened my eyes to show that, boy, I was going wrong somewhere. My life was being like in a storm, riding in this whirlwind, whipping at everything that was coming with it and tearing it apart.

BROADMOOR, 2001

People ask me why you end up being a drug dealer. I drew the short straw. But what people don't realise is that someone's got to run the street. The street men has to do it. If there were no street man there would be anarchy. Can you imagine if there weren't no drugs to be supplied to the fiends? They'd all he taking their own lives, killing. Ever seen someone have no drugs before? When the down from heroin kicks in the morning. They cannot function without it. You need the one drag, or the jab, or the whole of that fix just to feel normal again it is sad. Tell you something people say smoking cannabis is not a drug. It a medicine. For stress, pain, anger. It chills you out, it helps you deal with the cold slaps of life in your faces. It don't turn you into no madman. Coke and heroin that is a different ball game.

AGED 19 MADNESS

It was all getting a bit mad again on the streets around Stockwell. And then I get a letter from Star in jail and it's pretty to the point. "Matty, you never visit me Suck your mother. You're a pussy." I was pretty vexed and I tore up the letter. Why he writing letters like this to me for? To tell the truth i don't think my head has been the same since. I was thinking all you done for me is left me your business. Anyway there wasn't much I could do then because he was in prison, won't retaliate right now, sort it out another time. But he went and told everyone that he'd slagged me off in the letter and that I was too chicken to answer back. Soon they all knew that in the letter he was dissing me mum, and saying stuff like "you're poomy, you're boomy. You're afraid," It got to me. I won't deny it. There was pressure on me. What he was saying about me was playing with my mind. I tried to stay out of it, to ignore it butt was sucked in so deep into that life that the smallest criticism from one of my friends hurt really bad. And I ran round thinking that if it comes to the crunch then. Calmed down a bit the next day and went to see him and took him some new jeans in prison and some draw Star said Bucky rushed him in the showers in prison. He also had news for me. It was Bucky who had shot me in the leg that time in Peckham. He was serving time for robbery but he would be out soon. That's when I decided that I had to get Bucky for what he'd done to me. 51 Dandy had recovered from the shooting but he ended up in fail waiting trial for conspiracy and blackmail to get money for the show. Spliffington was put in witness protection and Pepper was in jail for selling cocaine, keeping DANDY on his feet and protecting him. And him, Larder and Toes and I heard they got a beating by the screws and this is when my world started collapsing.

While Dandy was waiting for his trial he also had a job for me. "Spliffington is an informer. I want you to shoot him "So now I got two hits. So I said to myself sort it out and he told me what date he was going in court, so I went to court with his brother and news reports cameras were out there it was like some show and I didn't know what was going on so I put on a hat so they couldn't recognise me and I had a gun and it was adjourned and everything so I saw the car and started following it and it went round the bend so I thought I'd take a short cut so I tried to reverse car but bashed it and jumped in and reversed and thought it was going on and I didn't want to get involved. The Spliffington business was becoming too complicated. Forget about it. Don't get involved. Then Star came out and I gave him back his phone with all his clients on "Here you go. It's yours. You run business. I'm tired of the game." Anyway, I started getting involved in the mobile phone business, selling on stolen phones. I just walked away from the crack business to try and do something more legit Then, out the blue I got a call from Natasha I'd stopped seeing her for a while was doing my own ting and I guess I'd neglected her Then she called me. "Come on over." I was with my friends. They all get hyped and started teasing me. "She wants you man." I thought about going over there. Trouble was the police were raiding the area and had a piece on me. "Fuck that shit man. I'm going home to bed and sleep by myself." I didn't want no trouble with the police. Why would I wake up in Stoke Newington the next day with a piece on me and no car coz me mates had if and the police bopping around? That was what I was thinking about at the time. Now I think back about it I was just Stared. I didn't want to go there because I was getting too close to her and it was Staring me See sometimes the brain of a woman can always see the wrong thing in a man. If you want to find out something about your enemy send a woman to them. When a man has sex and he feels good he reveals his secrets. Sometimes I seek refuge in a woman. Talking to them give me a sense of relief It's like a double edged sword. Women and love. Now, that's a double edged sword. Coz it can make you feel weak when you seek refuge. That's why I was kind of cruel to women, The way of life I was living. It was hard for me to show girls love. Love in a way to show that I really loved them. It was more like abuse I used to have hard sex with them to release my frustration. Most of the time was unprotected sex. I wanted to have loads of babies so I live on. I live on. Maybe I should have stuck with her. Maybe she could have helped me with everything that was about to park itself at my door. Instead I hooked up with a girl who was definitely wrong for me I was at Jennifer's house and went out to Coldharbour Lane to see Blood and brought some weed and this car pulls up and Tasha leans out the window "Matty, what you doing out here?" She was asking me questions about whether I'd heard anything about guy who got shot at Pegasus club in Hackney and would I talk to a guy called Orange. I was short with her. "You talk to him yourself.' She was trying to get me involved in her stuff and I refused so I walked off and left her there. Then Jennifer was trying to coerce me into having sex with her. I didn't want to have anything to do with her. I just didn't fancy her and Jennifer was getting on my nerves coz she was going I'm going to whip your arse in bed but I'd never ever shagged the girl but she talked me into it like a fool. Girls messed you about. They caused you problems. I brought Jennifer to my house and she stayed till 6am and we made some toast for breakfast and then I dropped her off at home. This will never be a one night stand." Then she went on. "I'm so good that if you don't like it then you are a batty man." And when I got ill I had all these batty man thoughts,

She kept telling me she liked me. It was nuts and I had some weird skin disease on my leg, like eczema where I shagged her. I don't know what it is. I saw her on the streets and she looked o my eyes and I looked away and it was like she was bragging that she was better than me in bed. As it was all going on I started dreaming about Natasha. I was dreaming about having nice, passionate sex with her And wet dreams. I wanted to left her how I'm trying to change my life and was ready to tell her that I wanted to settle down with her I got there and she was surprised to see me. 'What do you want?" I put out my hand to take her hand in mine. "Don't touch me," I was talking to her but she didn't want to know °I've been thinking. I'm falling in love with you. I keep dreaming about you." But she didn't want to know. I went back home and I start to think that someone is playing tricks with me coz my mind has gone a bit soft. But the thoughts persisted and in the end I had to do something about it. I called her up. "I'm coming over." "No. Don't bother. I don't want to see you." I was getting all confused. She must have seen a certain look in my eyes. "I told you not to mix with those people, come on man you gotta get over this." Her neglecting me didn't stop me. I put on a smart jacket and nice trousers, bought six red roses, hopped on a bus from Brixton to Hackney. I got lost coz I wasn't used to the buses around there and it a bit comical coz I was walking down the road with a bunch of roses and jumping on and off all these buses. It wasn't a common sight in Hackney and everyone was looking at me. And all I could hear was this voice in my head, you poor thing, you are in love. That's what I'm getting from their thoughts. And it was like everyone was pitying me. Why are they saying this about me? Why are they all condemning me? I get there and Tasha opens the door. 'What are you bringing these for? What are you doing?" 'What's the matter with you? I can't bring you roses, now." It didn't go well. Five minutes later I'd jumped back on the bus and sat in tears at the back of the bus, stamping on the roses on the floor, I wanted to talk to someone and the only person I thought could help me wouldn't give me a chance. She just wrote me off. And then Tasha found out that I'd been seeing Jennifer and this other girl and she wouldn't have anything to do with me. She wouldn't let me touch her. I pretended not to care.

I even convinced myself. But my world was collapsing around me.

BROADMOOR, 2001

As a man you got to be respected and be respectable. You gotta treat people well and treat people how you want people to treat you. It's about making a destiny for yourself. There is a generation of men who think that if you just sit down and pray everything will come to them. But I don't want to be like that. I wanted to go out there and make a stand for it and make my mark in life. The male role is to look after your seeds. Bring up the sprouts, make sure they go in the right direction. It's harder being a black male in a poor environment. There's always stereotypes you're supposed to follow like a gangster, drug dealer, Yardie. I'm a young man with ambition and willing to make a stance in life and take a position. Growing up as a fatherless child makes you have two things, not to fear life and death and it makes you a Leader. I don't even know who he is. I put my faith in God. "Though I walk in the shadow of death he will see me through.." Does my dad know

I exist? I don't know. I don't know what is going on. I was like some .secret baby. I have a picture, a quick flash of it, like I've been at the scene, like I'm a gifted child. Dad has to be there for their children. I got kids out there. I'm not there for them so I don't know what a real father is. I can't ask that question. It's too powerful. As a black father you've got to struggle. You got to be willing to struggle. They are under a lot of pressure from life so they smoke that weed. Don't want no one telling me how to conduct my life. I will work it out for myself. That's what happens when you don't have a father. So much anger and despair and hopelessness towards my feelings, my true feelings. My dad dishonoured me in some way. He left me to face this world like that. I've never seen his face. I know the publicity I had after the crimes. If he made contact, where is the love for his son? My mum says my father is dead but I don't know if it is true. Butt think she said that to close the book I want to know where I come from and what drives me. You see, I got my mother's heart but t don't know where my mind comes from. Not knowing who my father is has always been very painful, especially when your mum don't tell you. Who is this man? What has he done? Why am I the person I am today? In some way I feel like he is a powerful man. He must be because of the way my mind is. It's just too much to comprehend. I know my mum worries but what part my father played in all this, in my activities and all that. But my mum won't let me know about him. I don't know what he done to her or what happened or why she has got this attitude towards him. The thing about growing up as a fatherless child, you become the man early and you have to make ends meet and look after the family. You have a dilemma because you have to play the father role and it becomes difficult for a little boy.

AGED 19 (cont'd): BUCKY

Bucky was out and he was making a point about shooting me, bragging to people that he had shot me in the leg, boasting and showing off. It infuriated me. On top of all the madness going on the streets as the Hackney boys. Peckham boys and Brixton boys fought for their turf there was Bucky It was a fast mixture on street. What I wanted to ask Bucky was, "why didn't you shoot me up front then? Why are you such a coward?" With all the adrenaline going on and the drugs and the paranoia I decided to go for him. My mission was to get Bucky for the shooting and for what he had done to Star in prison. I went all over London looking for him got Dids involved. So we are driving around in New Cross and Peckham asking people but we didn't get anywhere. So we went after this guy called Benga. Who was this guy from Hackney and who was a big time shit dealer and he was hanging around with Bucky and he knew Bucky shot me so he was directly disrespecting me.

So I thought I'm going to deal with him too. Anyway we went to Hackney, kidnapped this youth called Skinny 'Where does Benga live?" 'Can't tell you mate " Dids got in the back of the car and slapped him around 'Where does he live?" That did it "OK I'll take you there". He took us to an address in Hackney, got out, and there was someone there but he wouldn't come out so we had to shout across the door Where's Bucky?" "Don't know" "Come and talk to me man." 'No, no. What do you want him for?" 'Well I was gonna shoot him, 'star." Anyway he wouldn't come so I drove off looking in Hackney and all the pool bars and stuff and couldn't see him. In the end I got hold of Skinny "Tell Benga I want to buy some shit off him." So Skinny was talking to him arid Bongo and his mum came out of the house. "You come to shoot me'? Well get away from the house or I'll call the police' And a few moments later we hear the sirens of the police car. So, Skinny man run off and Dids ran off with the gun and the police came 'What you doin' this side of the river?" They knew I was from south side of the waters because Benga told them. They questioned me, searched me but because I had nothing on me they could do nothing. They just wanted me out of there. "You got twenty minutes to get back over the other side of the river." I jumped back in the car and saw Dids walking along the road. "Where's the gun?" "I threw it in a bush?" "What d'you mean you threw it in a bush? Go and find it." "I don't know where it is" "Go and get my fucking gun." So he goes off and he starts looking in some bushes in someone's garden. Eventually he found it and we drove back over to south. I get pissed off with this cat and mouse game. Everything was dodgy. Even Dids was dodgy. I think I was reckless. I was too keen to be at war when I should have just got into money making it was all becoming pressured and stressful. My mind was beginning to go I started kidnapping people and I kidnapped Buckey's girlfriend. Tomica. We climbed through a window of her house and waited for her. When she arrived we grabbed her. 'Where's Buckey?" She was terrified. 'Where is he? Tell me or blow your brains out." "He's in Kings Cross." So a mate Pacman drives me to the Cross with Dids and Tomica in the back now and Dids who's supposed to be helping me is dressed in a white shirt, while trousers and red hat and orange peak "You going to shoot man dem dressed like that. In the night?' I didn't check on it at the time but you know, I think it was a set-up. I got the two fives in my waist and Dids, led me down a road and we parked up, leaving Tomica in the back of the car Dids was a 28 and he knew all the back roads of King's Cross. He was a player in the 28s and I was suspicious but I went that way with him "Come this way. We can sneak up on his arse this way." Anyway. I followed him but it was a dead end. I start feeling really paranoid. Something's dodgy here. And we stood there and as I turned round a police van appeared from nowhere. I never heard the engine or saw the lights, it was like a ghost. As he sees it coming towards us Dids made a play like he was giving something to me. I don't know whether he planted something on me or not. "What you doin'?" He didn't answer. The policeman came up to us. "You know you are in a drug zone and red light district what are you doing down here?" They said they wanted to search us. "I ain't got no drugs officer " Dids joins in. "What do you want to search us for?" And I was thinking, I don't know what kind of situation this is not an my turf Shall I pop these two cops now or what? What shall I do? What shall I do? I was seriously thinking of blazing the two cops. So I made a play and as the policeman came close to search me I push him against the van and ran for my life and I couldn't shake him off. I was running along all these terrace houses and everytime I nicked one bend and ran to the top of the bend he was coming round I thought fuck this. I took the gun out of my waist, wrapped it in a bandana and threw the gun onto a roof, took off my gloves and threw them in a bin and walked as though I was being normal. There was a helicopter flying around in the sky and sirens were going and all hell broke loose. This is a setup. The policeman had now caught up with me but I was still pretending I had nothing to do with anything "What you doing out here?" 1 was just walking officer "We saw you throw a gun on the roof." "That wasn't me." They didn't believe me and they brought me to the station and everything is videoed and they started interrogating me "Did you throw this gun on the roof?" "I don't know what you are talking about. I didn't have no gun on me. I don't know nothing about no gun." "Well you are going to court in the morning. Three firearm charges. Possession of firearms, possession of firearms with intent, possession of firearms and ammunition" They told me the gun had been involved in two shootings. I knew the shootings were done but I didn't know who done them. It was my gun originally but several people used it and it was kept in a shed on the estate. So, this is all happening at Clerkenwell court in Kings Cross. Barn I'm in the cell and they send this bloke in with me and lock him up too. I'm immediately on my Birdman and I'm sure they sent him in as a spy to get information from me Straight away lie starts talking to me "They said you had a gun and threw it on the roof. They said the same to me. Then they started beating me up Don't worry you will get out." I knew he was trying to get me to admit something but I just played dumb. "I don't want to get nothing from nothing that I ain't done." They led me out to the court and the jailers were giving me some lip. "You drug dealing scum. We always get you in the end." "Yeah, yeah, yeah. Whatever." Anyway, my mum and brother were in court and they'd managed to get the £5.000 bail for me so I got out that day I he only problem was that I had to sign on at Croydon police station at 7 o'clock every evening.

That tucked me right up. Signing on daily at seven p.m. The other conditions were that I was not allowed within five miles radius of Kings Cross and Dids. After I got bait I tracked him down. It turns out that he'd managed to make his escape in the mayhem of that night in Kings Cross. That's convenient, I thought. He was going on about getting my mobile phone if I got put away. Then I asked him what had happened that night and what he'd done with Tamica. 'I took her back to the flat and I was thinking of sexing her' I thought What is he going on about? I've got my case coming up and he's thinking about sex I was vexed that he was setting me up. I felt it Dids was setting me up and it was one big plot to set me up I moved in with my brother and he gave me a pump up bed and I pumped it up and he deflated the bed. That lasted a few days. So then I went to my mum's and left the Car outside and stayed there a few nights and then slept rough, But the police were always putting pressure on me. They'd always stop me. "Who's got all the guns? Where are the guns?" They were always on my case "You're the gunman aren't you? Where you hide the guns?" The stress of the case. The stress of living on the estate. The drugs. It finally got to me. And something cracked.

BROADMOOR, 2001

When you live on the edge the energy is burning up. Now I'm sitting here on the bed in my cell I can see them days as fun. Often I'll be thinking I'd rather be out there doing that than sleeping here doing nothing. Other times I get moments when I think fuck that madness. You know what it was like. It was like people were watching the blood sports and I was doing the blood sports. It was just a game for the rich people and politicians. What I got to realise is that they could control me, what's the word. Telepathically They've been telling me I'm ill and I realise that I'm not ill, It's been brought onto me. It's either a gift or a curse. One of the two. The scientist is he involved? No. It's bigger than that. There is some source beyond me. Some powerful shit beyond me. The place where "the scientist" said that two people are going to get killed lie did it to me. And made me act it out. Sent me on a destructive road. But the powerful source can only live if it's within you so you've got to chuck it out. So all the states of mind, some down to drugs, others to what has been going on in here. The game I've been playing in here. I knew I was playing a game when I came off medication. I can't say no more. And when I tried to do that I became ill and ended up in more trouble than I had before. When I tried to change everyone tried to dins me and say I was a fool. I got involved in old arguments and they were trying to bother me now when I'm not in the right frame of mind while I was trying to change my life and there was nothing going on for me and I'm not sure I'm not going out like that and I had nothing but guns going on. That's why I can't understand why I'm in this stupid place. It will come back in my face. I was in even deeper than trouble than I was ever before.

79

AGED 19 (contd): VOICES (5 months before the killings)

What with signing on at the police station every day and being banned five miles from Kings Cross made my movements were limited. It made it hard for me to make money. It was a struggle to make money. It was a struggle living so time felt precious. One day when I was dawn in Croydon trying to sign on at the police station, this woman brought in a lost dog. All I wanted to do was sing on but they told me I had to wait 45 minutes while they dealt with the lost dog. "You're taking the piss." I had just come back from visiting my cousin who was in jail for firearms and I'm looking at the future he was in for murder and I was in for murder. I just lost it at the police station, cussing and swearing at the police and at the woman and her lost dog. The police didn't take kindly to it and rearrested me for abusive behaviour. They searched me and found money and a £10 draw of weed. Then they started questioning me. "Whose money is this? Where did you get the drugs?" They put me in cell. The thing was there were cautions stickers Ail over the cell dirty sticky stuff on the wall. I was banging on the door shouting at them to let me out. 'What's the problem?" The problem was the cell was disgusting. They took me out and said they'd put me in a clean cell. All they did was just turn over the mattress and fumigate the cell and throw me back in again The fumes were intoxicating and I was becoming weaker and sicker. Finally they brought me out for questioning by one police officer and I told him that I wasn't a drug dealer and that I worked for a mobile phone company coz that was my cover for the drug dealing. But they kept on going on at me. 'What about the drugs? What about the gun? We know you are the 'gunman. Eventually they bailed me so I jumped back in my car and parked it outside my brothers, which was where I was supposed to stay as condition of my bail then got a cab to my mum's.

I felt ill and my belly was fucked up so I had a bath and went to sleep. In the early morning though I got a phone call to go partying, It was Forty and MBD. They arrived in a convertible and told me to get in the back. But the back seat was wet. The roof was down. It was freezing and I was sitting on a wet seat. They were taking liberties. What the fuck are they doing. We got in the club and this man came from nowhere and was dancing in front of me and trying to sell me crack and I felt like kicking him. I don't want to smoke this shit was pissed off about the wet seat and so I told Forty and MBD to drop me off. And MBD was going on about his family. "Everyone wants to be like the Balfours." And it was just pissing me off being around everyone so I started to stay in. I was worried about this case. So I started telling them "Selling coke is the devil's business " "Go away man, you're crazy. You are going crazy man." "What do you mean I'm crazy?" This when I started arguing with them all, over and over again and they think I've cracked and I think they are doing the work of the devil I got this thing in my head that selling crack was wrong and I started preaching to the young kids. Younger 28s started getting involved and I thought they shouldn't do it. I thought it was wrong that older boys encouraged the younger ones doing it and selling crack. So I'm saying I'm going on my jungle raves and smoking crack is the devil's dandruff and selling crack is the devil's way_ I was preaching to my friends and we felt out. 'Blue. We got the estate locked right down. We're making paper We've got a good business and you is coming out with some silly business Anyway, I never trusted Dids after what happened at Kings Cross. I see him walking one day so I chase him and caught him and he held onto groove of car and I'm pulling his legs and trying to get hold of him. I'm trying to pull him into a corner and stab him up and that's why he was holding on so tightly. I hit him with bottles, everything. All the time Dids is talking to me. "You shouldn't have done that Matty." I started punching him and kicking him but he was still hanging on and meanwhile my friend started pulling him and the police swarmed the area and so I jumped in my car and headed to Norwood and chilled out and told my brother the story. My mum got a sick note from the doctor. She could see that I was ill and I didn't have to go to Croydon. I was preaching more and more to my friends. I was preaching abut the bad things we were doing. In the end I thought 1 don't want to go to jail. The voices started small at first. So small that I didn't recognise them as voices. Just voices suggesting things to me. Judging me 'Why d'you do this?" "You're going to pay for it." My mum saw what was going on before me. She got a note from the doctor saying I was mentally unstable and wouldn't be able to sign on at Croydon police station. I was supposed to stay at my mum's in Brixton and at my brother's house in Croydon The shooting case. The stress the police were putting me under...The phone shops they raided and they took all the documents and don't know what they said but the next day I went in and they were all looking at me like I grassed them up and no one said a word to me all these yardies in there. But police put me under a lot of pressure. I didn't want to cooperate. They were saying You are a gunman. Where's the guns?" Every time the police stopped me there were always gun police around and my money was going down fast because I had such an expensive lifestyle. Weed, drink, petrol. It was going down fast. And I was going with it. It was like I was failing. I wanted to get away. They broke the firearm case into three charges. I wanted to get this case out of the way. I wanted to know what would happen to me. So Forty said he'd help me.

He wanted to take me to a clairvoyant, an African man who could predict the future And I thought I never been to a scientist in my life and decided that I wanted to see my reverend who was going on a missionary trip to Africa and make him pray for me and I had a bad thought in my mind I thought if I go to Africa with him I can bring back some heroin. So I think he got wind of my plan and wouldn't let me go. Then I thought right. I'm going to Jamaica. But somehow I couldn't leave. Something made me stay I wanted to break out but I couldn't So in the end I agreed with Forty's suggestion and he took me and Tally to a house in Lewisham Tally went in first, then his mum. Then Forty. Then it was my turn. "He'll see you now." I go in and there is this man with tarot cards and he turns them over and starts talking. "I see lots of loss of money. One death. Two deaths, two girls playing around with you None of it meant much to me. 1 was trying to figure out who are these two girls "Get rid of all your trainers." That was another thing he said. It was absurd. I must have had about 40 trainers. I thought, no way am I getting rid of all them Then he wanted a grand as payment I was out of my depth really, What am I getting into?

Anyway, I left but he wanted to see me again. I was worried by what he predicted. I thought some of my family was going to die. I told my mum what happened and she took me down Battersea to a reverend. This man looked in his crystal ball and he flipped. "This is too soon, too soon." That's what he kept saying I turned to my mum 'What's he talking about?" "Don't worry son, it's nothing " And the man went on. "He started too young, he started too young." The only thing I could work out was that he was saying I was smoking too much crack cocaine from too young an age. From the police station to the place where Roger brought me and the place my mum brought me I've never been the same. That's where it all begins. That night I slept for three days at my mum's place and during this sleep, I dreamed from present back to when I was a baby. And when I woke up I felt weak like I'd died and come back to life and the world was different I went to step out of bed and the TV clicked on and a TV presenter shouts. "He's made it." I thought what's going on here? What the fuck is going on?

BROADMOOR, 2001

When you are born your destiny is written out. Flow many more have that destiny? There were some of who were the same as me and I don't know when I will see them. There are others who followed my footsteps and got into drink and drugs. All I say to them is "be careful because the law will try and grab you and put you behind bars "When you are behind bars you will see how fake people are. There is no such thing as love. There is conniving, jealousy, envy, plotting. The devil's on the streets. But God is in us so reach out for him. God is in everyone but the devil runs the streets. This is how I rap it's freestyle. God's in us but the devil runs the streets so watch out before he swipes you off your feet. Make you hit back, make you land in the pan so check it out before I write this with my pen. God's in us but the devil runs the streets black, dark rainy beats, hear my style because I'm so unique. God's in us but the devil runs the streets. Fuck the bitches, quick riches, and kill the snitches, Oh my gosh, the devil runs the street. God's in us, please repent your sin.

AGED 19 (cont'd): JUDGEMENT DAY

From that day I woke up the voices just got louder and stronger and stranger. It was like a permanent judgement day for me. I hear some voice in my head going "Why did you do this?" I replied, 'What the fuck you talking about? Leave me alone." Then another voice was going, "Don't worry about him ' I stayed inside at my mum's and stopped smoking crack but the voices got worse. Then they drove me mad it's like spirits were judging me. All the sins I done in my life and I was being judged by them. Every little crime, misdemeanour, was corning back as voices. Spiritual judgement starts coming, You got to be punished for things you done. Angel on one side, devil on the other. "Why did you do this?" "I don't know: My body was changing as well. I didn't feel myself. 1 found myself sitting at my mum's crying with incessant voices in my head, "Why you treat that girl like that? Why you steal those drugs? Why did you take that gun?" Was smoking more and more weed to stop the voices. I was sitting on my bed thinking, why won't these voices leave me alone? And all the time the voices are talking to me. "Your mum is trying to poison you. Kill her." During the day I would watch sit in front of the telly, day after day, watching the politicians in Westminster on TV and f would watch them to see how they sit and what they were communicating. And depending on how they sit I would react. Sitting with feet apart is like a king. So these voices kept on going on and next thing I know John Mayhem is communicating with me on the TV. The thing is I was aware the whole time and I kept thinking, this ain't real this is nuts. My brother come in once and started saying things to me "See that big circle and the small circle? Well you are the small circle." Thought what the fuck do you mean? Get out of my room. He was driving me mad. And then it was like, what's going on? I started having these out of body experiences, like spirits coming into me like the devil coming in and having sex with me. It was painful having sex. I'd be in bed and I'd hear the voice command me. "Open your legs I'm coming in." There would be a whooshing sound and I'd be all confused. 'What are you talking about'?"

Whoosh, and then he would be straight up my arse. And it would be so painful and so real I'd be on my hands and knees with my belly and chest pushed into the air. I was trying to sleep and it would just happen. There was no one there. It was the devil. I was screaming. It was like the Exorcist when the girl's head spins round. There was this woman I thought she was doing it all to me. If I looked through the window there was this African woman watching me, playing with her hands and I was thinking she was working magic on me and doing my head in. And I thought listen, leave me alone and it was like someone set mons onto me. They were Tugging me and driving me crazy and in the end he goes to me, the good voice goes "You got a lot of bad things. Get rid of them and I'll make you a rap star." I thought yeah, that sounds good. So I went outside and told my mum to get all my money from the bank and every day I got a bundle and started handing out notes to nieces and nephews and friends. It was £20 here, and £10 there and £50 and £100 I went up to people and said, "here if you want it take it.' And it went on like this till my money ran out. The voices are driving me crazy, good and bad and telling me and teaching me things. I start venturing out back outside and see the big moon over me and there was no one around and I can't see none of my friends and I go to the corners where my friends used to hang out and there's no one there and I'm listening to the radio and I listen to Rise FM and all these pirate stations on the raft but they are talking to me, directly to me. Don't cross the barrier " it was because when I looked through the window of my house I saw these wooden barriers going up and I thought that's what they meant. But I did cross the barrier and walked down that road and I listened to this radio DJ Chris Goldfinger and he starts threatening my life. The people on the radio start threatening my life So I sat down and got taught by the people on the radio about how to communicate. 'If you cross your foot to the right you're communicating with the police. If you cross your foot to the left you are communicating with the Home Office," That's what they told me. They also said something else "If you are in trouble or in a situation, you cross your foot and someone will come to you and you will get away with it." This is what was going on the whole time as I'm sitting my room smoking weed. I was trying to figure it all out. 62 And one day I got out of bed and said I was going to Tasha's house and there was this big red arrow of clouds pointing to the tube station. It was magical and I started following the clouds and I bumped into my friend Serge. He could see I was a bit out of it. Where are you going? "I've got to check something out He invited me into his car to smoke a spliff and in the end I smoked a couple of joints and never ended up going to Tasha's. That'd be the kind of thing that was happening to me all the time. Every time I wanted to chat with a girl like I normally did they would look at me. "Go away You are crazy Go away." Everybody seemed to think that I was crazy but all I could think was what the fuck is going on here? It was terrible I had no female warmth for months. And I just kept having wet dreams and my back was pumping and I started reading newspapers and there were messages saying "you are going to be a rap star and there is a party over there, go there.' And all the time I'm being judged and assessed by these spirits. In the end it got so bad that these voices started telling me to kill my mum and telling me bad things about her. Then one day I was in my room watching this TV programme about a priest molesting young boys and at that very moment my mum came in and said she wanted me to talk to someone. 'I've got someone I want you to speak to." I went in and there was this Reverend. He was a bit poofish. And again I was confused. What the fucks is going on? Does my mum want to set me up with a gay reverend? I should kill her. I got so mad I kicked the TV screen in and it wouldn't break so 1 got something and smashed it and it exploded in smoke and I threw it on the floor My mum came in all horrified. "What's going on? What are you doing?" "I don't like what I'm watching." Anyway now I'm thinking it's better for me to leave now because these voices are telling me to kill her because she was setting me up with a gay reverend. I went round to a friend's house who was in prison and his baby mother let me stay the night. I stayed up all night in the front room watching TV. But even on the way there I had this fight. This man came down with some keys in his hand and I thought he was inviting me into his house and he was a bit queerish. "What the fuck are you doing?" "What do you mean?" "Fuck off" "Oh come here you fucker." Then he kicked me in the shin and as I grabbed my ankle he went to hit me but I hit him first with an upper cut. I swear to God I mashed him right up and I swear to God he flew off his feet, but he picked up a bottle and ran after me so I ran down to Brixton and I wanted to get some youngers to petrol bomb his house. In the end I stayed at my brother's, just praying. I think someone sold my soul to the devil and I was praying for my soul to come back. That's when my mum took me into hospital.

BROADMOOR, 2001

I think I live for the adrenaline buzz coz you know you are alive. When you are in tight situations you have to think quick - zoom - the adrenaline comes in and it's a movement. TV is very powerful It's a movement. I think of adrenaline as the power of God, it's like the power of the spirit. It's the movement of the people But I like chilling as well. I think things are going to work out for me though I just need a bit of patience. This is what I want to say. I'm not criticising anyone who picks up a bag of drugs to sell because their baby is hungry or their family is poor. You know what I mean? It's a struggle. Life is a struggle and if it was a just world there would be no need for all this. It would be harmony. So it was created like this. Sometimes you are forced into moments that you have to take action and do things, but all I'm saying it is the way that God wants it to be and I don't think it's right. Selling drugs and carrying guns isn't right. Somewhere along the line the devil is playing tricks with us all. Even while I was in the life I was praying. That's why I am alive today. I've read the whole bible now, just for me. And when you lead the bible it makes you see that in the New Testament you've got a great sinner. In the Old Testament, that was the way of the mankind from Adam and eve and the apple business. Even if you sell drugs and carry a gun it don't mean you are going to hell. They say Christ died for our sins and so all it takes you have to believe in him and saying his name to save your soul. That's why I ended up here. I was going deeper and deeper and getting more dirt behind me until I was stuck.

AGED 19 (cont'd): WAR

My mum could see that there was something seriously wrong with me. I was out of control. She took me to the GP who sent me straight to St Thomas' hospital. I thought we'd gone there because I had back ache. I didn't want to hear about no mental illness started telling the doctor my symptoms and he's writing stuff down and writing and writing and I'm talking. "My back's hurting, you got to fucking do something " Then I grabbed the paper he was writing on and tore it up in front of him. He pressed the alarm and several people came in, held me down and jabbed me. I woke up two days later in Southwestern mental hospital. I've been out of It for two days, I woke up all confused and came out my room and looked round and thought, oh my God what am I doing here? It freaked me out not knowing where I was. I found a doctor. "Listen, I got to get outer here. I don't like here - It was winter, coming up to Christmas and I was freezing I didn't really know it but I'd been sectioned to 28 days in the hospital. Anyway the doctor says I can go out for a couple of hours arid walk around, so i head back to Stockwell and all my friends are there and they tell me I look much calmer and better. But even then the police are still stopping me on the streets asking me all sorts of questions 'What gang are you with?" 'Where are you going?" I felt they were winding-me up. I head back to hospital but I know that I want to leave straight away. – The place was dirty and there were down and outs and I was locked up and I'd never been locked up before It was horrible. A nightmare. That triggered me off a bit. I just kept thinking, What happened to my life? Why am I in this down and out place' I thought, these people just want to keep me in here Anyway, the doctor said I could stay out for the weekend It turned out that they didn't have many beds anyway so I was doing them a favour.

So I went home and met up with this girl who was this friend's sister and I thought about sleeping with her but my mind was wandering so I got up and went off to find Star on the other side of the estate. Star was up on his balcony so I had a spliff with him and my head started hurling like it was frying. What kind of weed you try give me man?" But before I could take the accusation further there was this car beeping down in the street. I look over and there is Rattle in his car and he shouts up to me. The gun I borrowed you is in the hole in the wall." We kept this 38 in a hole underneath the stairwells so I went down put my hand in the hole and pull out the 38 and put it in me waist. And then Star tells me he's going on the road so I go off with him and we find Billion smoking weed and the police are all around. I'm getting paranoid now and I'm in the car with the gun and there are police all around and I try to get out of the car but the door won't open so I get even more paranoid. What sort of set up is this? What the fuck I'm a sitting duck." I'm thinking that they've set me up with the gun to get arrested. Fortunately Billion arid Star came back to the car and drove off. But I'm realty paranoid now so I think I'd better stay away for a bit. But later that day I head off to Mixers this club on Stockwell Road, the gun still down me waist. I moved to go in but they wanted to search me which got me irate they can see I mean business so they back away and I get in there without them searching. It's now about 1 am on Saturday and it's a cold winter's day. I start drinking some drinks there and it tastes to me like piss so I throw the glass on the floor and walk off And Smoky is outside in his car and he gives me a spliff. And as I'm standing there I see these weird guys walking towards me. Where'd they come from? They were licking their lips at me so I started firing the gun at them. But they didn't drop so I look at the gun. What sort of gun is this? Then I try and fire at some petrol tanks on this lorry to see if they explode like in the movies but nothing happens, they wouldn't go up. The gun seems to go off but the tanks don't explode. I must have been hallucinating coz no police come and no one seems bothered by me firing the gun. So I went back to the club and the bouncer there again starts hassling me. "Have you got a gun on you?" And I pull it out and show them. "Look it's empty." Suddenly chaos happens and they lock the door and smash bottles all over me and punch me give me a black eye and I'm still holding the gun and they are trying to get it and they grabbed the gun and opened the door and threw me in a puddle And I'm mad with anger. Why are they starting on me when my head isn't in full health? Fucking hell.

They've got me right on my own doorstep. I'm in a right state so I went round to my brother's house and I don't know whether he's called the police or the police have come round but suddenly I'm in handcuffs and taken back to the hospital. And the police refuse to take the handcuffs off until I've taken the medicine so I take the medicine and fall asleep. So I wake up two days later on Tuesday and I go into the day room and ask if I can leave and they let me out again And that's when it really started. The voices are going to me, "kill, kill." They mentioned specific people but also general people The message to me was, "Injustice has happened to you. Now is the time for revenge." It was really like the end of the world was coming, apocalyptic. The world was a desperate and dangerous place and t had to survive it. Like back in Viking days. I just ran with it, Fuck It if this is what they want then I'm going to do it I saw the message on the billboards. On TV I heard the politicians talking directly to me. They are all saying the same thing "Go out there and kill. Go on. Go and kill." It made me go mad and made me flip. It was like the end of the world was coming to me and this is the time that only the fit and strong survive and in order to do it you had to stay strong and get back at all the people who had done me wrong. Injustice had happened to my life. It was more about revenge and anger and what happened when they beat me up that turned me crazy. But even in the midst of all this I'm still thinking, What is this stupidness? But then I follow the other voice again and doing what it says. Madness. Fucking hell. It's going on and on and I'm in a mad house and in the end my head just went Boom. I played the game. I went to war Over six days I shot dead the bouncer at Mixers, I tried to shoot my mate Star. I stabbed Bob, the Italian and Steve. And on New Year's Day I stabbed a Lady to death.

BROADMOOR, 2001

Serious times man and it's getting worse. I don't want' that again walking on the street watching your back. There's too much to life than that negative activity. Right now I wish I could be on the beach and drink a Guinness near the sea shore watching the sexy girls walk past with my daughter nearby and I can visualize that and be happy with that. The only place I been is France and I never been to Jamaica. I know a lot about America but never been there. I was offered to go there but I turned it down to do crack. 1 was a fool to myself. Maybe if I had them experiences it would have changed things for my longer time. But saying that, who knows why I never went? In his destinies are played out. I made it my destiny because when I was in the station I confessed. My head was gone. I was shell shocked and I couldn't handle it no more. I was gone. If I stayed out there I would have killed and killed and killed and killed. And it would have been terrible_

AGED 20: THE AFTERMATH

What's happened to my life? Where'd it go? I was trying to make a way for myself - When the killing happened I was gone. The Matty I thought I knew, the one who I thought I understood was long gone. He was tortured and thrown out of the body and he's been fighting to get back ever since. They put me on remand in Feltham and as I went there in the prison van I was thinking, boy, what have I got myself into? It was a new hell about to begin. They gave me an induction and you wait to see what wing they will send you to and I was in there and ate my chips and beans and all that but they had nothing else, no smokes, no magazines, so I stood on the table and addressed all the scared young boys who like me were waiting for their wing 'Where do you come from? Come here. What you got?" I pat them down and take their stuff and I done it to the whole room. And everyone coughed up. And then the screws called me. "Hutchinson come out." And I came out with magazines and tobacco and Walkmans and I walked to the screws to get my brown jeans and denim shirt and black shoes and I was arguing with them. 'What are you going on about? Can't I keep my clothes?" 'No. Take it off.' This big Italian guy came bursting in and told them that I'd nicked his stuff. So they put me in a box thing, like a small cell with a chair and not much more. They locked me in and took me to , the hospital wing and there I had this cardboard chair and a little bucket to piss and shit in. Fucking hell. I thought saw these guys Young and that in there and Titch was out working in the yard driving a tractor. I came out for some food and this white guy was there and he had a Walkman with a radio and I never had one of those. "Let me borrow your Walkman with the radio and I'll pay you with some tobacco" So I had it now and he walked off and the screws came and said I robbed him. Next week my mum, my brother and Jeddy came and they brought me some clothes but the screws wouldn't let me have them. I got some weed off Jeddy and cheeked it and the screws searched me as I left the visitor's area but they didn't find it. After that I put it in me pocket and this Chinese bloke came in. 'Have you got any matches?" And I said "is that your girlfriend?" And then he said "if you think you're bad, come to my wing " And I hit him and banged him and the screws came and took me to the hospital and after a little while I went in front of the governor. "How do you plead?" "I don't plead guilty to nothing." You are charged with possession of cannabis, robbery and assault."

The Chinese guy was there grassing me up and he was the one who was giving me an earful. They gave me seven days solitary confinement which meant a loss of food and privileges. So I was on the block now fucking freezing and asked for jumper coz I still didn't have some clothes and they gave me a little jumper that didn't go past my elbows so I had to do exercises to keep warm Then they took away the mattress in the morning and gave you a bucket and brush to scrub the floor but all I used to do was kick the bucket all over the floor and make it wet "I ain't scrubbing no floor" There was this guy called B Smith and he was arguing with me all the time. "You are a pussy".

Then I went back to police station for three days questioning and there were fourteen charges on me, six, no seven for GBG, three for murder and attempted murder and they put me on an ID parade and when they told me what I'd done I was visualizing all that was happening "Yeah, that was the bouncer's girlfriend wasn't it?" It was like a dream when I was remembering it and then the Marlorr Snapes "That was his sister wasn't it?" They said yea, How did you know that. And then this policeman called John Balchik came and started questioning me and he was going, that Merc is in the car park and I will give it to you and he was fucking with my mind. A third party was there but he sat there and didn't say anything and my solicitor was there kicking me under the table and he kept saying, "say "no comment"." But I confessed for the simple reason that I didn't want to live that life no more. I confessed. I told the police of new crimes. They promised me the world. The next day they put me in a cell with some stinking tramp who smelled of piss It was hell that period. I got beaten up and felt pure rejection. I needed time out to sort my head out. Sometimes I think, I should have just lied and skipped the country. And then I testified to all the crimes they charged me with, some of them got dropped because I was chatting rubbish I told them where the gun was.

They took me to the house in a van. It was some house in Streatham. That's where I used to keep the gun. It was a house with seven apartments and the landlord just let us run it and my friend used to run parties there. His name was Belly. He got phone calls to tell him to move the gun but they moved it to another plate, but they found it. It soothed everything when they found it. They took me to Feltham in a van, I was on K2 bully wing and had an argument with some guy and next time they moved me to Belmarsh CAT A and I grew a mustache one day and shaved it like Hitler. No one liked that. They put me in a cell and threw a mattress in there and kicked me like an animal. The mustache provoked them. Anyway, this Irish guy called Denver. I don't know why he ain't here now coz he was mad, he goes to me, "Hutchinson if you want to get out, smash up your cell " I didn't know anything about prison so I listened to him and smashed up my prison cell. Then all the screws came with riot gear, shouting and everything. "Surrender." They screamed "Surrender what?' I said. They made me get on my hands and knees and say surrender They bend me up like a package and put me in a padded cell and poked me and abused me and I saw them around in uniform and attacked them. In Belmarsh it was just fighting and fighting and they kept beating me up. My mother and brother came to see me and I was in a harm proof suit with bare feet. I hadn't showered for a week and I'm faced with them in a little room and I picked up a chair and whacked him with a chair and the screws were there and that was the end of the visit. A few times I tried to run off and smash up my cell. I was shitting and urinating blood. They were serious internal wounds. And I was just in and out of this pink padded cell thinking should I kick off again? I didn't eat, I stopped eating for nineteen days coz they kept putting stuff in my food. No toilet nothing was just moved from padded cell to the shower, then back into a padded cell again. It went on for weeks like that. That was a helluva experience Then they told me I was going to hospital for assessment. "You are going to Broadmoor." "What's that'?" 'It's a hospital prison." It was a terrible place. Loads of zombies walking around. I got there and wanted to go straight back to normal prison I thought that if I acted up they'd send me back. There was a guy called Dr Morson there and he was always clicking his knuckles and I wanted to rush him but they put me in a cell before I could do anything Then I got my chance with this female doctor called Lisa. I spat in her face and the nurses rushed me and they pinned me up against a wall and I had one of them by the throat and we are fighting, Two on one arm, two on the other arm and they were trying to grab my legs and they pulled down my pants and gave me an injection and I was out for three days and then they let me out in my socks until I met a few people and then they put me back in seclusion. Then I got let out and" was given a room and it was stinky with a big hole in mattress Then before my trial I was back in Belmarsh. The trial made the news and everything. I thought I would bust the case. One of the witnesses got killed before the trial. But I don't know nothing about that. The whole case blew up. With guns, helicopters. The criminal fraternity came to court and testified against me. The same lot that wanted me to sell drugs to them testified against me. School friends came and said their piece, all the gangsters came to crucify me The whole thing just frightened me maybe coz I was full of medication but the whole time I didn't feel myself. I just prayed and felt frightened. I was frightened by the whole situation I thought my god what have I done? I got six lite sentences, and a minimum of fourteen years before parole. But in October 1996 my solicitor appealed and got section 3741. Diminished responsibility. I was sent to Broadmoor. Broadmoor was crazy. I was put in Ronnie Kray's old cell. I was in the same wing as the Yorkshire Ripper Peter Sutcliffe, and the Stockwell Strangler. Kenneth Erskine. Sutcliffe had a smell of death about him. It was like a cold air was surrounding his body the whole time. He sent chills down my spine. One time I walked into the unit and my mate was trying to strangle Peter Sutcliffe. It was Kenny Erskine, the Stockwell Strangler who pressed the panic button That's how mad it was in Broadmoor. And its been Broadmoor life ever since.

BROADMOOR, 2001

In that midst of madness the good voice was talking to me saying give away all the dirty money and the bad things and you can become a rap star. When I got to Broadmoor I thought that if I was gonna be a rap star then I'd better practice and it became a test of the voices to see if what they said were true. So bought a stereo for my cell from an Argos catalogue. Before it arrived I started praying. "God, if this is meant to manifest make it have a mike socket and let me practice it.' And you know what, it came with a mike socket and I thought, yep this is to be. 1 was just singing 'yippee, yippee, yippee yah' over and over again to start with. And I was singing that for hours. Adding little bits to it. But to tell the truth it weren't much good and f got so frustrated. I was listening to albums and I couldn't find nuttin' to rap about. But then it started clicking and I began to rap. It took time to manifest but it was true it's funny init? Its unbelievable. It's like a fairy tale, man. It's like a fairy tale, I learnt to rap my life. Don't waste your time about judging me, let's get to a thing called reality Someting was up, something went down, something went wrong and something turned round Now I'm back in physical form to be a number one MC So give me the rights to my freedom you see, my liberty to rock the party Let's get to the pad, the mission and plan, that's the one with mike in hand Not the one with gun in hand, tell everybody you must understand Hoggy Dog is the man with the mike in hand That's the one they call Blue, of course he's got the biggest stones so true So what we gonna do? We're gonna scoop him up in the back of the truck and take him to the VIP spot And after that we're gonna give him a notch of brandy, hey it makes us so lovely Now I've gotta stop that game of selling the bone because it causes too much pain know I've gotta say something more, coz I know I've got to score Drinking liquor is a nice, nice thing, I had that from 1974 I wish I could just have a bottle of that gin to kick back on all of my sins now I've got to testify, on the microphone I rock it like high, I'm thinking of rocking the spot in a nice white suit or a belly hat I don't know about the game, all I'm talking about is a piece of fame so come on doctors and nurses, don't be no crazies don't be no jerkies just get off your ass and give Hoggy Dog that famous bus pass, straight out of Broadmoor and onto the stage for he is going to get paid and any girls that need laying that's okay, my life is now back on form locked down for seven mother fucking years, looking through windows and bars and stairs all I wanna do is get out in the sunshine please God give me a dime on the mike While I spit these flows tonight Because I'm so hypnotic they say I'm psychotic All I say is km so hypnotic coz I'm gigantic on the mike MCs, everybody in the cool is listening to me What's my name? I've got the lyrical wisdom and the lyrical facts to let you know that G9 The niggers am crazy, they sit on crates, they drink beer and they steer If anybody comes from the rear, they are kicking and booting and smashing into the ground because he's from out of town, don't batty around Hip hop it can't be stopped you know how we do that, we chew that From the back of the brains to the microphone to know I'm not insane my lyrics are like wisdom, like that, they go "pow". Then you know I'm not so slow oh gosh, I'm the illest in the click, can you hear my spit? These rhymes they are like bullets they're coming down so you better bow down now the Dog is in town. Since 1977 I've been on the mike wanting to reach heaven rapping and rhyming rhymes, talking in my mind thinking about things, but now I've got the illest style in the click oh my gosh, my mouth is like a ball It spits rhymes and it spits them out like bullets "Pow, pow, pow" to your face, jerking your body, making you shake your waist stamp your feet on the dance floor, because I've got to score drinking liquor on the freeway. coz I've got to get pay because you know it's my day And it's still double G and do not play Tell 'em to leave me alone And let me get on the microphone For me it's all a part of the hustle. The hustle can't stop. So I got to put it into music. I got to rap my life. Like I say it's a fairy tale. The good voice was true all the time I learnt to rap. It's like a fairy tale.

AGED 33: ENDINGS

I gotta keep on persevering even though I'm in deep waters It's an ongoing fight. I been through many different moods and minds in Broadmoor. Broadmoor life has been hard. Many people have died here. Frank Bell, rest in peace. He was one of the closest to me. The staff at Broadmoor hated him because he give as good as he gets. Tim Slater, Mad Dog. Alex rest in peace. Hanged himself in front of me man. This is a serious place. In 2007 they said I was less of a threat and moved me to the Royal Bethlem Hospital. I'm still on medication. And hopefully I will get out one day soon. But I have to keep on praying and repenting for my sins, connecting with the far one and healing myself and redeeming my soul. I shed many tears and it's a way of pouring out the sins in your soul. I shed many tears At the end of the day I have to take the responsibility of killing these people. It's like if I keep on putting the thought in my head about what I did it will turn me into spaghetti. I have to try and overcome it for myself and ask for forgiveness and I've expressed my feelings in prayer about the people I killed. I said to them "I hope you rest in peace and I'm hoping I can connect to you through a better place." In order for me to make any progress I've got to learn to overcome that and look forward. If I keep looking back it will kill me. I remember when I was trapped in the midst of it all and they said, "Do you know what you did? You killed two and injured three. - It cramped me and I never washed and never cleaned my teeth. For a year in Broadmoor, that first year all I did was sleep and stay in bed smoking in my room and it was Jules, my mate who said "you Have to overcome this I tried to call on the Lord for help. It was just one hell for me. I am sorry for what I've done At the time I wasn't in the right frame of mind Two wrongs don't make a right. Killing the woman was madness I pray to her and ask for forgiveness. And Freeman, one of my stabbing victims, I heard he's just died of cancer. I feel like he's got to a place before I've got there Life's a journey and he's Just got there before me R.I.P I've had good times and bad times, but the bad outweigh the good. People have forsaken me and taken liberties and every dog has his day and mine will come one day. The good times in my life have all been about smoking and drinking and having little sessions and little parties and listening to music and relating with one another. There've been good times. And I can't have these good times in here no more. Like it's forbidden now. I have to move on and grin and bear it and soldier on. I'm following footprints. I just go on. Sometimes it feels like hell on earth. I feel like something dark has grabbed me and imprisoned me. But sometimes I think it wasn't the devil that put me in here. It was God that put me here. He might have a message for me. Take a stock and look at life and don't take things for granted. Though God knows why it happened to me my personality is changing since being here. I've become more civil, more understanding. I want to say to the kids growing up, stay in school, learn your books and try to strive for a high position as a job and so black people can rise up and stop the negativity " And I want to tell everyone else, 'Be honest with me. Speak the truth. Don't try and bullshit me and we will get on quite fine." After all the madness, the mayhem the confusion I still got my faculties about me. It's a good feeling.

Understanding my situation. That's what I want. People say I have schizophrenia. I have got schizophrenia it's not a nice thing at all. I just want to get some freedom now and see my family and get to know 'em want to get to know my kids. I got kids. I don't know how many off spring I've got. I've heard I had five but I'm not 100% sure. I want to find out what's going on in their life's. No one is telling me shit. Course I would like to know who they are. So I can be their dad and play that role, I know for sure I got a daughter. Rachelle. She is 15 this year. I speak to her every now and again, but the mother don't get on with me so I never seen her. I got a picture of her in my room though. I don't want no more kids. Maybe some digital babies so they can't kill me. Family. I got things like that on my mind. Not spitting stones out of my mouth on the roadside saying "Twenty pounds, twenty pounds" The rest of them, the G's are still out there doing what they do. I don't keep contact with any of the others.

I'm just in here, taking it day by day. Waiting for judgement day...

Redemption

The arrest and the first week of my incarceration.

3am I woke up on 1st January 1994 surrounded by Police. I was taken to the station. My mother, my niece and my nephew were at the house. When I got to the station they said I was arrested for the first murder of the year. I was interviewed by John Boucher, Maureen Boyle and an independent appropriate adult. In the interview, no comment, no comment, no comment they said to me "Tell me who done the murder and we will let you go, tell us who, know what I mean and we will let you go, you know what I mean". No comment, no comment. The next day I was sent to Feltham. In the sweat box I met someone I know from when I was growing up, name G. he was on his way to Feltham. He got taken somewhere else, I got put into the main reception. After court I had fish and chips and sat on the bench and said to myself bloody hell I am in prison now, where only the fittest of the fittest survive. I stood on the table and robbed everybody in the room, I took stereo, smokes, magazine, cards, everything. I was of course allocated to a wing then. Then a guy kicked off and said why you bloody bastard I'm going to get you, to kick you in the head, fuck him. They put me in this little box where you sit down near a screen. Suddenly I was put into the hospital wing. I was put in a cell with paper chair and paper table. I sat there, I was the stressed. I thought (bloody hell) then they found everyone my mum, brother and Belly they brought me in a joint of weed and had a chat with them. On the way back in, I was waiting in the waiting area, waiting to go back into the hospital wing, had no matches, I know where I can get some matches, I smoked my weed. There was this China guy came looking, I was like you got some matches? He was like you think your bad or something? I cuffed him and knocked him out. I was arrested and sent to block. By this time I had put the weed, in my pocket. They found the weed and I was sent to the governor the next day. I got done for fighting, cannabis and sent to set block for 7cc, down the block. I was there waking up every morning, exercising and reading the paper, each day like it was T.V. My old colleague I knew from dealing round New Cross passed me some weed now and then. I had an argument with some young guy. The next day screws said this, they are taking me back to the Police station. I was in the Police station for 3 days, by this time now, thinking about what I had done and how I felt. I felt sad. I felt bad for what I had done, and I knew that if I got free, there would be no change in my life because the state of my mental state was really bad, no one really knew how unwell I was, only myself. I hid it and portrayed to be acting normal and well, while my mind was playing tricks on me. Got to the station John Boucher was interviewing me and he said look people are coming out of the woodwork about you, they started telling me about incidences that had happened at friend's houses, around the neighbourhood, with peers that I grew up with and all the information they were telling me seemed to be the truth. They were coming out of the woodwork talking about me. Many families who I grew up with and called friends, street people, and rogue people. They broke the rules and started informing on me. So at first I was saying no comment. So this time I was eating food in the station, because at this time I had no food when I was in prison and I hadn't had a bath for the whole week I was in there. I had a shower, my first shower since I had been away. I was eating and my head started hurting me and I was getting these headaches and the voices are getting worse and louder. I said I need help I can't go back into the community like this and what I have done is very bad and I don't want to live with this on my conscience. So I got annoyed to know that the people I grew up with had betrayed me and they all pretend they don't talk Police and they don't work with Police. It hurt my feelings, really sold me out, lots of them. Many families that I grew up with, I won't mention no names because they know who they are. We don't need to be vindictive and name any of these people, they know who they are, they know what they done and they are still organising business up to this very day. I ain't living that lifestyle no more. They say two wrongs don't make a right. So I was interviewed again with Maureen Boyle as my solicitor from St Meredith and an appropriate adult. So John Boucher is questioning me saying all these things before. So I said look and started to explain why I had done the things I had done, these crimes, and I was very upset and aggressive about it. I said look I did this stabbing because he tried to rob me. I done this shooting because I was beaten up and I was being bullied and threatened, you know I was just defending myself and I confessed to all the crimes I was arrested for and crimes that I never done, even murders that I never done. I just wanted to be locked up so I could get my head together and sort out my life because I wasn't in a good place. The interviews went on for three days. I told them where the gun was. I just confessed. I threw in the towel. I wanted to be locked up for what I had done. I was sent to Feltham back in the block more arguments. Till one day they came to me and said look starring you up to CAT A. I said what is CAT A? This was all new to me, so I was sent to Belmarsh. The first day in Belmarsh I was sent to the hospital wing. I didn't like it. I was in my cell and there was this Irish guy that kept on bothering me, telling me I must fight or telling me to get out of hospital. Misleading me. I didn't really know any better because I was in the jail and I didn't know about prison life, but I didn't listen to him. So when I had a shower I came out, shave out my beard and my moustache that looked a bit like Hitler. I was going in my cell and the nurses started grabbing me. I was like, "what are you doing" all I want to do is go to the house cell block 4, I don't want to be down here, they beat me up and wheeled out my bed. I thought fuck it, look at this I haven't even fucking done nothing and I'm getting ill-treated. So the next time they open the cell I knock one of them out. I was beaten and thrown back in my cell. So the Irish guy next door to me said look Hutchinson, if you want to get moved, smash up your cell. I thought that was a good idea. I didn't know no better so I smashed up my cell. Kicked off the sink, kicked off the toilet, water flying everywhere. It brought the MUFTIE SQUAD after me, the armoured, masked guards. They said I should surrender and I said what I have got to surrender. So I faced the wall, put my hands behind my head and got on my knees. They ran in beat me, grabbed me. Brought me to a padded cell, stripped me naked and started punching me up. I was in there for about 3 days. Then they put me back in the cell with no bed, just a mattress and a fire proof blanket, in some rip proof clothes, bare foot this was going on for about a month. My sister got permission from the Police to come and see me.

She said don't you want to get out of here and see your friends one day? I said what kind of treatment is this? Every time she came they made me come out to play pool to make it look good. See they had me banged up all the time. There was one time where the door was open and I tried run off the wing. I got grabbed by the screws beaten up and flung back in the padded cell. Then one day my oldest brother and my mum came when I was in the padded cell. They took me out barefoot, I hadn't had a bath for about 2 weeks now. They said you got a visit. I said mum look how they got me. I was on a visit barefoot and my foot was black, my skin was all chipped up and bruised. So I just get a chair and whacked it over the head of the screws and that was the end of the visit. They beat me up again and then back to the padded cell. This went on for a month a lot of beating and fighting with them, till one day I was in the padded cell and they came up to me and said right you are going to Broadmoor. I was like what the fuck is Broadmoor. I said I don't want to be in no hospital. They said you're going. I was going to kick off, but didn't because by this time I was shitting and pissing blood. They took me to Broadmoor. I met the medical director and some nurses. They had me in there cracking jokes about me how they been beating me all the time and how they had me. They put me in seclusion. A doctor came to see me, it was female doctor and some nurses. I thought I don't want to be here so I am going to kick off. So I kicked off and spat in the doctor's face, they started fighting. It took about 20 minutes and they eventually got me and injected me. I got knocked out for 3 days. I kept on waking up, looking in the team's faces and then falling asleep. I think in the back of my mind I heard my mum talking about these places. How people come in here fight, get injected and never come out the same. From that I thought I am never going to kick off with staff again. It was a hard road. I was released from seclusion after about 5 days. I thought what kind of a place is this? People walking around not banged up, sitting down in chairs watching T.V. They said to me "you want a menu" I said menu, menu for what? Your food. I was like what kind of place is this man? So I started filling my menus and eating. They had this Trinidadian nurse who was working with me. It just seemed weird. People started talking to me. I just reserved myself and kept myself to myself, saying yeah whatever. The first time ever I met a black gay guy was there. He was trying to be friendly with me all the time. He said his name was Jordon and his Dad was a Police officer and he had been brought up in care and he was in there for about 100 burglaries. I just started talking to people. I met some Bristol guys I started kicking it with them. I met 2 other guys from Brixton and they were the main ones I was kicking it with. I started to get more visits, getting more weed and smoking and sharing it with the lads, but I noticed the weed was making me very paranoid, you know. And then I was taking some tablets they weren't making me feel great, they were making me feel tired. But I wanted to go to the gym. So then I went to my primary nurse Andy and goes I want to go to the gym. He said if you want to go to the gym you got to be on a depot. I was so keen to go to the gym I took the depot that was it. I was just in the chair, sitting down sleeping. They wake me up for meds. They wake me up for food and then I go to bed. I was like that for a few months. Then this new doctor came, called Dr Payne and started questioning me. But I never let anyone know what was going on in my head. You know I just kept my thoughts to myself. I didn't really trust no one, I didn't open up. I'm thinking like where am I? What is this? Why am I getting an injection in my bottom? It is a violation it just seems weird. He started talking to me, I said look I never done nothing wrong the Police stitched me up, I was trying to get out of this situation. They kept on questioning me, if you never done it and I believe in you, you can go home if you win the case. I was like wow man I really need to get out of here. I don't like it here. My family are visiting me, my friends are visiting me but they seem Alien. I was 20 at this time. I was always on the phone making calls to girls, friends, family, trying to find out what is happening. And people are trying to tell me what has been said or done or whatever happened. I was just trying to find and work out what has been happening but the medicines were making me really tired. Every morning I got up early, I had to get up early and get dressed and be in the day room for 9am. I had to play this Bob Marley tune on the stereo. I had to blast it whilst I was getting dressed. Because I was very upset and the Bob Marley song was singing "please don't you rock my boat. Because I don't want my boat to be rocking anymore". I played it and the staff just left me alone. They must have thought that, yeah he is going through it. There was this nurse called Kerry who took a liking to me. She started bringing me in music and talking to me, having conversations with me, which was helpful. She had a little daughter and we would talk, you know. She would bring in magazines for me. The Source. We got on very well. Some of the lifers there were from prison after serving their sentence and they were annoyed causing mayhem, there were a lot of fights. My behaviour was good, I managed to get on well with myself. There was an American guy there called Frank, he said he was a body pop champion in New York he was really good at it. I was just getting along with my peers. A few of them smoked weed, I would sometimes smoke weed and have a chat. Then one day I was using the phone and they said Ronnie Kray is coming down. I said why is he coming down to use the phone? So by the time I came off the phone the whole ward was locked up and Ronnie Kray was there. So I came out of the phone room and I saw him and he goes you alright son? I was thinking that you are not my Dad. You shouldn't have got a life sentence, appeal against your sentence and try to get a section you will be better off. I said ok. I walked off. And I was thinking why is he calling me son? I thought much on it and thought, no he ain't my Dad. Anyway, he used the phone and I went to my cell that night he went to sleep and had a heart attack. I prayed to God about it. Ronnie Kray died of a heart attack. I thought this is madness, madness, and that is the end of that. And then they said to me I am moving to the higher profile unit. Where Sutcliffe, and Ronnie Kray was. I was like, look I'm 20, I don't want to be with them guys. I don't need to be with them. The guard was like you are high profile, you gotta go there. So I went up there. They said they would take me in handcuff if I don't go. So I had to go. When I got up there I met loads of guys, some cool guys. They had things kinda under control. They had Hooch, opium base ash coming in, cooked when we wanted, watched videos till late and go to bed. We were there smoking the stuff and the staff would stay in the office. We smoke, drink, eat food. I would have 2 jays and I would be off my head, then go to bed. They would look at me. I would say alright and just go to my room start training and go to sleep. I was on remand for about a year. I think I went court on about 9th February. The case was high profile. The witness in my case got killed and that made the case just blow up. When I went to court there were helicopters, 2 Police cars at the front, 2 Police cars at the back, from departure to the Old Bailey in 40 minutes. The traffic was stopped. I was tossing and turning in the back of the bullet proof van. It was on the news. It was in all the papers. I thought my God what have I done? When I went to court, I sat there and watched all these people I grew up with fabricating stories, just to make me go down. I couldn't believe it. I thought these people, I stood for them. Grew up with them. Got love and respect for them and they're coming and testifying against me. School friends, older guys, I just sat and watched it all. The medication I was on just numbed me. I didn't know what was going on, what is this? You know. I had one option to win the case and that was to make my Mum lie for me and to swear on the holy bible. In the end I thought I can't make my Mum do this. I've got to face my justice. I have just got to do this, so I said no I don't want her to testify. I got 6 life sentences to run concurrent with a minimum of 14 years, but I thought the Judge said 40. When I went back to my cell, I thought fucking hell I will be out when I am 61. Then the jailers ran down to the cell and said Hutchinson, Hutchinson, no, no, no, don't get it twisted, don't get it wrong, its wrong, its wrong, it is the minimum of 14 years. I thought wow what a relief but 14 years is a long time. It was court 2 of the Old Bailey, which is where the Kray's got sent down too. So being put in Henley ward, after all this time fucking about. There is this doctor called Dr Taylor, she is a tall Caucasian lady with ginger hair and after the first time she saw me she had a big split up her skirt and she crossed her legs and I could see all up her legs and she just kept on talking to me. I was like what is going on here? She took me off all my meds and that was a smart move as I was alright. My mind weren't that bad, I had some paranoia thoughts, but they weren't that bad. Then one day Dr Morrison called me to the office, because this nurse John wanted to spoil the party. He was a nurse who'd came back from leave and wasn't happy about what was going on and with the intention to break up everything.

They called me in the office and said "are you happy here" 3 meals you getting a day, I said my Mum used to cook for me. Ok so after this discussion you will be sent to Banbury ward. I said what is that then? He said the high dependency ward. I said what am I going there for? He said you are going to pack your stuff. When I got to the unit there are a lot of sick people. Very sick people. I thought, I felt a bit sorry for them so I gave them all my cigarettes. They smoked them. I asked them for one and they told me to fuck off. I thought alright that is what kind of play this is. So I ordered some more cigarettes and kept it moving. I would sit in the chair with my headphones on blasting music and watching the ride every day. You sat in the day room from about 9 to about 6 in the evening. I would sit there and sneak off to the toilet and now and then smoke my weed. And just sit there and the whole ward would erupt. Chairs, tables would be flying over my head. People getting stabbed with pens, hit with table legs. I thought fucking hell this shit is madness. I need to get off this ward, I need to get out of this hospital. I phoned my Mum and said look Mum I am on a life sentence here, I'm not taking this, I'm going to back to prison. I'm not taking this one moment longer. I can't handle this, this is madness. She goes son if you don't stay there, I'm not going to visit you in prison, I don't want you in prison. I said Mum I can't stay here. She said you do that, it's up to you. So I was contemplating going against my Mum wishes now. After all I have been facing the music myself whilst she has been supporting me. I don't want to break the bond now. Shall I appeal to go to prison? Dr Venulan, which is the doctor on Banbury was the closest asset I had there. There was a nurse there called Ian Forshaw, he kept coming up to me saying Hutchinson, Hutchinson you horrible person, you pulled the trigger, you are going to do 20 years. The man kept on winding my up, winding me up and pushing my buttons till I'm going to smash his face in. when I was getting close to that, I got a call from my mum. A lady was also on the line saying that her husband was in there. She said look my husband is in there and if you fight them, they are going to kill you. So I said to myself what am I supposed to do here now? This man is on my case fucking pressing my buttons and I can't do anything I must just take it. So I was like no man I can't handle this and he was on my case. He kept on coming and coming, coming, coming, I thought fucking hell. One night I sat in my cell and thought to myself, what am I supposed to do here, I can't do nothing I am powerless and I contemplated suicide for 3 days. Then I thought to myself fuck that, to the people who would like to see that. It would break my Mum's heart, break my family heart. I'd listen to the Bob Marley song. Someone gave me the legends Cassette and it was redemption song, you can free yourself from mental slavery. And from that song, it gave me the fight to fight on. That thought was erased from my mind. I thought I have to get strong enough to deal with this. I wanted more and more weed to escape. The weed was putting me in false sense of security, a coping mechanism. It wasn't helping me, I didn't like the feeling it was giving me though I requested it more and more, till they said to me. You are smoking weed and they banned my friends and family from seeing me apart from my Mum and sister for one year. And I couldn't get no weed. Only the little bits that people would give me and they were so mean. I didn't smoke it like that I put a lot in, they putting in specks, they saying I waste it. So I was getting pissed off about this, but I managed to get a bit of skunk here and there but that weren't nothing that I liked. Then from Banbury I moved to Mendip ward, Dr Gosh it's been about a year I have been on a section and I applied for a Tribunal to get out. They said I wasn't ready for it. It made me feel sick, it broke my heart. Bloody hell now these people got me in here they don't want to let me go. I was put on a tablet called mineral, mineral or something and I was constipated for 2 weeks and I was hungry so I kept on eating and eating. And my belly got bigger and bigger and when I went toilet it was like having a baby I was in so much pain. I told the doctor I am not taking it anymore and she took me off it.

I would like to talk about when I was in my first term in Prison, in Belmarsh, because of my treatment for 19 days I never eat no food. I would take no medication. I never saw no wing. After being sent to Broadmoor Luton ward I was put on medication Clopiczole depot 500mls it knocked me out. That is when I spent all my time on remand on that ward. I was sentenced to 6 life sentences concurrent, for 14 years minimum tariff. The charges were 2 manslaughter, 3 GBH's, 1 attempted murder. I was on Henley ward now and my cousin wrote me a letter saying do you know Peter Sutcliffe, so I showed him the letter and he said don't worry about me that is just what they say about me in the media. The man had the aura of death around him. He had a cold breeze. You smelt death when in his presence. I told him I didn't like him and I wasn't scared of him, I am just a simple lorry driver he said. On Henley ward now there was a guy called Penee he wanted to be famous for killing Sutcliffe. There was the Walworth murderer and he also wanted to hurt Sutcliffe. I met Kenny Erskine, I was 21 thinking my God my life was changed for the worst. I am 21 look at the prospects now, I am in Broadmoor with all these serial killers. There was a guy called Jay and a guy called K, I got on well with them and became friends. As I said we used to smoke and drink and the Walworth murderer said he would hurt Sutcliffe and Penee would hurt Sutcliffe. After I got moved Penee strangled Sutcliffe with a cord and almost killed him, but Kenny Erskine saved him by pressing the panic bell and they left him semi-conscious on the way out. So he got sent down to Banbury ward and he told me the story of what K wanted to do to Sutcliffe. They arranged to stab Sutcliffe in the eye to blind him. K stabbed Sutcliffe in the eye. He done it with a felt tip pen. It blinded him in one eye, but he didn't achieve what he wanted to do, he wanted to take out both eyes. He ended up on Banbury ward. When I was on Mendip ward, as Ronnie Kray said, my solicitor Paul Graham said yeah he was appealing against sentencing and that was to drop my life sentences and to get a section 37/41 a Home Office restriction order. On November 1996, I went to the Royal Courts of Justice in front of 3 red robed judges and my sentence was turned over to a 37/41. Whilst on Mendip ward I had my first Tribunal and I lost it. I got into an altercation. I got moved to Banbury ward that is where I met Dr Venulan again. But prior to that Dr Venulan came to court and said I will do 10 years in Broadmoor to help me get off my life sentence. I was on Banbury ward it was crazy. Many crazy people. I'd be there talking people out of suicide or harming themselves. Whilst the staff were mostly in the office chilling drinking tea. I'd be amidst of all these patients, talking to them the craziest of craziest ones. They were talking to me going on, they were good experienced people and their life just went wrong for them and they were very ill. The ones that were saner were bad. They were fighting and arguing and disruptive. I spent about a year down there. So I kept myself to myself. I kept my weed to myself, I thought fuck it is my weed and I was just keeping it to myself. Eventually I was moved to Thornton Ward. Dr Venulan's other ward, he ran Banbury and Thornton. Me and the other patients got on well. At this time I was getting education, studying, Maths, English, Computers, Word processing. I spent most of my time in the education centre. My medication was changing from one thing to another, to another. They were saying I was untreatable and I would never get better. But in my mind I would never believe it, I just said this is a phase I am going though, that I would overcome. In the midst of this I was fighting my demons, I was reading my Bible. As I was reading my Bible I would hear them talking, I would curse and curse and read the Bible until they would go away. I read my Bible about 8 to 10 times a day. And I knew it was giving me solace and strength. I would talk to my mum every day and she would tell me the problems she was having with the family and people she was getting in situations with in the community since I had been away. She was my rock and I was her rock, you understand me. You know the family had kinda turned against her and was harsh on her for sending me to Broadmoor. There were things what happened to me that led me there. My brothers and sisters, one of them was more helpful, one was a bit helpful, my sister was there now and then and she came to visit me all the time I was in Broadmoor. Every week she would come and bring me food. And she would help come to my meetings, but I think she didn't really understand the situation because she kept on agreeing to change my medication every time it wasn't working and the medication was making me hallucinate, see things, hear things. It was really having an adverse effect on me. You know it was trial and error. Sometimes I was good for a while and then sometimes my head was gone again. I remember one time going to court in a bullet proof van just before I was going to the appeal. My friend brought some crack for me and I smoked it in the bullet proof van on the way to court and they were going what is that smell and I was laughing, like look at them. Smoking these dirty things in the Police van getting to court in armed procession. That is the last time I smoked it, it didn't agree with me and I made a vow to stop smoking it. It was crap.

I travelled from Broadmoor to Belmarsh on the 19th February 1995 under section 45/41 of the mental health act. I was described as very aggressive, psychotic, low intelligence and thoughts uncut. Unintelligent about fighting. After they said I was deluded I believed I was number 1, the Tiger in the jungle. I was hearing voices from the T.V. and the radio. My sisters describes me as the sole of the party and don't suffer fools gladly. I was recommended by the social worker for psychological training, but I never took none. And the psychology report indicated I didn't feel I needed to speak to psychologists. The forensic report said I had no index offences on being arrested, only one for firearms which was when I was returning from my girlfriend's house. I was stopped by the Police in Kings Cross and was accused of throwing firearm over a wall. I was bailed at my sister's address for £5,000. I had convictions for Cannabis from the 13th January

1993 and 13th August 1994. After insulting words. I was mainly prescribed surdelete, but it never made me be stable because I was smoking Cannabis and it didn't agree with cannabis. Then I didn't feel well again. I was prescribed Olanzapine and that didn't work so they decided to put me on Risperodone. I had a Nigerian solicitor who tried to get some good independent doctor to back me. I had this doctor that was from Landor Road, a senior lecture consultant psychiatrist. I booked him Opuko Orizano he recommend on the tribunal that I have a deferred discharge because I was responding well to treatment and they placed the specification that I should be resident at a hostel and compliant with antipsychotic medication if considered. Abstain from illicit substance to random drug test regular. To be fully access to community psychiatrist, social worker and health care to visit me at consultant outpatient clinics. Dr Gosh said that I understood everything and that was the end Tribunal in 1997 I lost it and I was upset. I think I prayed and prayed and prayed. I even fast, never eat for 10 days fasting. I was heartbroken. I was positive, but I still kept on praying.

Let's talk about a Tribunal I had July 1st 1990 I was psychotic I was on Banbury ward, anger, frustration and my past history and my experiences in Broadmoor. The frustration, you know, from the Police station, what I heard. From what happened in the community. Two wrongs don't make a right and they were two wrongs. You know, but it left me angry. And when I was psychotic I went to this Tribunal and the wind was blowing. You know, I just went in there and said look I don't want to go home because I kill people, you know. They were like why do you want to do that. I was look at all I am faced with in my life is shit, you know shit. They was like sorry to be this way, but this is how it is. You have got to learn to handle things. I said, so that is the situation are you going to let me go home? Turn the telly on, you know the report. I waited until October to get back that report. And they said you are not going home. You have to be detained because you are mentally ill and psychotic, deluded in that present state of mind I thought they were being honest and truthful. But that is the way it is when you are psychotic and deluded, in truth you are not right. It might be the truth to you, but it is not the truth for reality and righteousness, you know. And I was upset, but that is something and I think anyone that don't understand anything I just said, when you are psychotic, you are psychotic and when you think you are right you think you are right. That is Schizophrenia for you.

So with all my experience of Broadmoor, there is a valuable lesson. The staff they did not take no talking there was a strict regime. The staff are all like soldiers from the war and they came back from war to work in hospitals and run the hospitals so it was a very strict place. There is leeway, there is some that is good and bad, there is some that will be on your case and some that will help you out and you know relationships were made and rapports to get through your situation. Some were stricter, some would help you. Yeah was I was always getting in altercations for using the phone, because I was always using the phone. Phoning home, phoning a friend. And they said I used the phone so much and when the recorded phone calls came through, they said you could only talk to the person on the list and sometimes I would speak to someone who wasn't on the list. I'd phone my mum and talk to my nephew and they would say that my nephew wasn't on the list. I would say he is my family, he is my nephew and I want to talk to him, so that would cause problems. And they would say that they were recording and you are not allowed. They would go on and on about, but it is an unfair law. But what can you do. There were many fights. Violence was rife in there and when staff came they would beat you up and if you fight with them your pants would go down and you would get a needle in your bum. As I said I never fight with staff, as of on the first day I went there. So I held it down and conformed in that way. I had fights don't get me wrong, like when I was dealing my little bits and pieces people wanna have a go. Think I am vulnerable or whatever and it ends up in an altercation. Most of the time I was on reprimand I was worse than the person who start it because I thought they didn't like me and they were treating me wrong and unfair. But coming to realise the situation now my index offence was serious. And some people weren't in there for serious things. Maybe they were thinking I should know better or they were being hard on me to do better. That is what I see it as, I should have done better. I shouldn't have had all those debates and arguments and all those silly fights. I should have been more mature. I see that now, in my older and wiser head. They were pushing me to do better. Like the time I thought they didn't like me, you know. In the medication way of things in the BNF book early 2000 to late nineties I been on nearly every medication in the book. They said that I was untreatable all kind of things. And when they used to say it to me, I used to say to myself I know I will get better I don't believe that. Some of the medications made me have hallucinations, funny feelings in my body. Drugged up, speech slurred, tiredness, weight gain. I remember one day Dr Venulan came and said look you have been on all of the meds and you still keep on getting ill, so I want to try you on Clozaril it is a wonder drug, because if I do that, that is the one that can you get you discharged quicker. I was like no I am not taking that. Because if you take that, they have to take your blood every week to see how the white cells are in your body. You know your white cells, I was like I ain't going on that. Some people have bad reaction, they even died, I was like no. Months and months went by and he was like, try the Clozaril, try the Clozaril and I will give you discharge quickly. I tried it eventually, I got red alert and I nearly died. My white cell were like going, so they took my off the Clozaril straight away. You see the main thing is that you get red alert and you have to come off Clozaril really quickly you are bound to relapse. I did relapse and I remember I was in a meeting with my mum and they were like saying if he is stable on this meds we are putting him on for 3 months, we will refer you to three bridges. I can remember my Mum breaking down crying, saying look what are you doing to my son. And seeing my mum cry made me get upset and I started shouting and throw the paper files on the floor and walked out of the meeting. I was really upset to see my mum in tears. I thought look at this. Then I calmed down and they said look we are going to work to get you out of here. This is after I was on the Thornton ward, even after I was on a relapse from Windsor and I was on Banbury for a long time. Then I went to Thornton. This was what Dr Venulan was saying to me. So let me go back a little bit. After being in Broadmoor I had to get money. There were these 2 staff, I would gave them £30 and I would get 2 half bottles of alcohol. This was nice, but it really made me feel buzzing you know, especially after so many years. I would relax, sit listen to music and have a drink it was nice just to have that little chill out zone. And I was well into my music. I was always writing songs about my past life, what I was seeing, what I heard, you know. That is when Lord have mercy came out. I had many friends, I was very popular you know, the black guys I got on very well with them. Some of them wanted to fight me and bully me, but it wouldn't work like that. They cockneys, they showed me a lot of respect. There is one man I would like to mention, he passed away whilst I was there. His name was Tony Pilditch he used to sell jewellery, fix watches and any time I have had any trouble with the jewellery or watches he would repair it for me. And I would go how much is that Tony, he would say go on mate, you're alright, go on. He was an elder and used to call me corrupt, you know Mr, you are corrupt. Rest in peace Tony Pilditch because he was a good guy. Frank Bell body popper he lost his life on Banbury ward one night, rest in peace. Tim Slater committed suicide, rest in peace. And all the other people who committed suicide in Broadmoor. There is about 10 – 15 suicides in one year. You know, it wasn't an easy place you know. But I tried to make the best of my time. Sometimes I was depressed. Sometimes I was frustrated, but I kept it positive by reading my Bible and believing in God and keeping my faith and just remaining positive. And working on my music and going to the education centre and doing my learning and therapies. I done CBT, I done one to one, drug addiction work, alcohol work and I done index offence work, I done victim empathy psychology. I remember one guy, I had a CT scan, testing my brain. I remember, I have ECGs every year. I had a dentist that did like me and she used to call me every 6 months to polish my teeth. I had an ingrowing toenail operation on Broadmoor, but it wasn't done properly and I had to have it redone when I had left. I have to big up Tony Roach for the music he made with me. I have to big up all the staff who looked after me. There was one staff on Thornton ward, his name was Nick Harry. Every night he came in on a shift, he would bring in about 20 quarter pounders and fry them in the night and say, come on lads we need to eat the quarter pounders and make them nice, he tried to make it as comfortable for us as he could. He was my primary nurse and he helped me get discharged. He was a good guy. I would like to talk about Stan Grant the therapist who helped me write my book. He used to run a group, the black men African heritage. I did work with him for years, and I done the group with him and also one to ones. I was the second youngest in the group and I held my own in conversation. I was up with the forum. I kept my opinions, I wasn't subjected to any pressure or anything, I made my comments, if people liked it or didn't like it. It was no strain to me. I was strong in that group. I would like to thank Stan Grant for being there for me, he was a great ally and Cliff his colleague was a good support. Most of the lads I left behind and are still in there to this day. You know, I remember what I used to say to them. If you in your own house, and someone's goes to your own house they play by your rules, so if you're not in your own house, you are in the system play by the rules and just get home to your family. Don't get comfortable and think that this is life. There is more to life than that, you know, get yourselves well. Take your medication, leave the drugs out, because medication and drugs don't mix. I hope to see you guys all one day soon. And when you are out stay focused and do the best you can and stay away from drugs. That's it big up Duppy rass, Mr Mohammed, you know, I remember when, I was going through rough times and I was neglecting myself. I was at the early stage of the sentence and he helped me get a laundry job, you done all the work, I just pushed the cart and I got paid and I would buy you a little smokes as you don't want no money and that really empowered me to push on. So thanks Mr Mohammed, good guy. I would like to say before I went to Thornton ward the inquest came in about my index offence. The hospital named South Western, the inquest found them negligent. That I was neglected. They neglected my care and they took responsibility for what happened. It was on the News and my case became high profile again for the negligence. When my case came up, it because my case was high profile again, my phone calls had to be recorded, so I had to walk three blocks from the block I was on and go in the phone booth and put a tape in to record my calls. The only person I was calling was my Mum and I said is this really necessary. They said the Police or whoever said my phone calls had to be recorded. I phoned my Mum when she was in Jerusalem. She went over there when there was a war on and I was worried for her, because she went on a church trip. She said she was in a church, left the church, a day later gunmen ran in the church and the soldiers bombed the church with all the people and the terrorists in there. I said Mum hurry up and come home I am worried about you. She made it back and I thanked God for that. I was upset that I was ringing her and the phone calls were getting recorded and you know, It was really hurting my feelings and I was thinking that all this time and being here, after all this time of being here, like I am a terrorist or something. I was a young kid growing up on an estate. As you read from the previous part of my book, I had friends who were doing naughty stuff and naughty things when the shit hit the fan I took responsibility for what I done and the people I was associating with. Most of them said their piece. So, it was not like I was calling those people saying I wanted to harm them. I had a few friends. Girls I had casual relationships with before. I don't know if they were getting their own back but, I called them and spoke to them with no inappropriateness or rudeness, no threatening. I get a call from the staff saying the Police had called saying have you spoke to these girls and if you get caught calling them again you will get done with nuisance phone calls and get arrested. All I said to these girls was I hope you are happy and getting on with your life, and I thought why did they did that? Did they think it would break and I would kill myself? What are they trying to do to me? And it made me stronger. I realised that the people that I thought were for me, weren't' for me. You know. They weren't for me. Contacting the home office saying they don't want me to contact them, things like that. It made me stronger, so it was a waste of time. That friendship, yeah. There was one who said that she had my child, then it was not my child, then it was my child, then it wasn't my child. Well, it's not my child, because if it was my child you would have brought the child to come and see me, if I was father, so I know that now. And when I said that in the book I had a child that was 19 you are not my child. You know. Back to Thornton ward. I was on Thornton ward with Mr Campbell and a couple of guys where just there. This one night there was an argument, one guy was getting most of the abuse and he left and went to his room. Well, that it what we thought. But when I went to go and get a drink I smelt gas all over the place. He had turned all the cookers, hobs, the grill and the oven open all it would take was someone with a light to blow it up. So I told a nurse and they put a lock and tap on the gas and put it in a box and locked it. So they would turn it up if you were cooking and lock it. At night it would be locked. There were so many bad things you know. People getting stabbed in the eye. I remember one time on Henley ward a guy brought a deodorant lit it, burnt it and burnt Kenny Erskine hair off. Finally they banned deodorant. If you wanted it, it was locked in the cupboard you use it, spray it and lock it up from that day. One mad thing I remember people would be greasing up and then fighting officers naked. They would be covered in grease so they couldn't hold them and they were causing damage. Some people would get mad and get the cream and grease up and just run out fighting. After all these events now, they said if you want cream, you want to have a bath, come to the office and open the office go to the toiletry compartment use your cream and then bring it back. I was pissed at this law now, because being a man of colour, a black man you need cream when you bathe, when you have a bath. So this is going on now, I was having my showers coming down the corridors in my towel saying can I get some cream please. They were saying we are busy you will have to wait. By the time you had finished you were dry and freezing, because the place is freezing, people have got all the windows open so you freeze your bollocks off. You finally get the cream, you use some and bring it back. This one time I said I would not bring it back, they said you need to bring back the cream. I made a strong argument people of Caribbean and African descent we need to grease when we bath. Can we have this cream in our rooms because it is pointless. I am not greasing up and fighting everybody. I need my cream and worst of all the water was hard. So when I showered I used to get a burning itch a lot, so I need the cream straight away. Eventually it worked and we were allowed. One thing I want say is, where I am at this stage in my life the score goes down, I had them when I was hospital and Broadmoor. I was always telling people good advice. No one can say I was telling them to do something wrong or negative. Unless it was for some altercation. There was someone sorting it out. No one can say I was telling them to do wrong, I was always giving people good advice, you know, talking people out of suicide/harming themselves, abusing drugs. Some people take medication spit in a cup and the next person drink it. Taking this tablet, that tablet and mixing it, I said you can't be doing that kind of thing. Whatever was prescribed was for you, and don't want to buy some off someone, it is crazy. I never got into that kind of thing. The only drugs I ever took was Cannabis, as I said when I was going to court in the Police van that was the last time I smoked crack. So the thing I want to get to now is about Broadmoor, I had many Tribunals. I had about 6 or 7 Tribunals because you can have one every year. I got knocked back, knocked back, knocked back and I was praying for the day to get out of there. As I said a day seemed like a year in there, it was long and I was smoking tobacco, tobacco, roll up after roll up. Worrying about my family, my Mum. So I just want to get to the point where the day came when I got out of Broadmoor.

This was the Tribunal's decision from 10th September 2003. Wayne Hutchinson was admitted to Broadmoor on 13th February 1995 from Belmarsh. His diagnosis one is of schizophrenia. His condition is largely controlled by medication and he is fully compliant. He has a history of mental illness controlling symptoms, including delusions that he is a dog. He has no delusions since a brief respite in 2002 following an alteration in his drugs. His index offence was in central court in May 1st 1996 of 2 counts of manslaughter/attempted murder and 3 counts wounding with intent. In terms of life imprisonment November 12th 1996 appeal. An order was subjected to a section 37 together with a restriction order on a section 41. The offences I committed from December 1994 to January 1995 they include firing a shotgun into a victim home in the early morning in thereby shooting a of man public house by killing and slashing a woman in the face. The Police have put unprovoked stabbing, so he proposed the condition continuing detention. But as a result in particular are the CPA meeting that they said I should be in medium security. That meeting was really important, as a result to all parties that I should be transferred to Direct Lodge and they referred me to Fredrick lodge in Edmonton. Fredrick lodge to address the drug abuse. Following the meeting the Forensic psychologist and social worker, that this was right because it was the view of RMO writing the reports the patients is suffering from a mental illness to a degree and it is appropriate for him to receive medical treatment in a hospital, until for his health and safety. For the protection of other person. As evidence Dr Vernan confirmed that present view was simply it was his nature and it was appropriate for him to be detained in hospital. We found all parties were very helpful in support to go with the clinic team for the new proposal step. The view of social worker Mr Phillip supported that RMO he did not anticipate a problem finding a place within Fredrick Lodge. He certainly thought that their drug abuse treatment was the key. The view was also endorsed by the psychiatrist Stan Grant. That Mr Hutchinson is a damaged individual, damaged in effect of his substance abuse. We consider including all evidence that Mr Hutchinson we noted that he wanted to go the Fredrick lodge. He noted that it was better to go to a medium secure unit and have a conditional discharge at the present time. He recognised that he has a mental illness that requires medication. He said that if he did not take his medication, he would become psychotic. If he took illicit drugs he said would be set back. He repented for his past actions. He has very fully structured activities at Broadmoor. We are quite satisfied that he continues to suffer from a mental illness and that it is not his nature which makes it appropriate for him to be detained in hospital for medical treatment. We are entirely of the view after yesterday's CPA meeting and numerous evidence before us that he should be transferred ideally to Fredrick lodge for further consider that the transfer should take place as soon as possible. We consider it is essential for him to undergo further treatment addressing drug abuse. So we consider he should participated in structured activities that as is he is in Broadmoor. We recognised it is vital to continue to support that he has from his family. So in 2004 march, I was off to Fredrick lodge. What I would also like to say, in my CPA report my summary risk assessments. Triggers, types of triggers, vulnerability low. Self-harm and suicide low, harm to others and property low, fire setting low, abscond/escaping low. Inappropriate sexual behaviour low. Use of alcohol and illicit drugs high. Non-compliant with treatment low. One things they did say was the risk of me mixing with criminal associates they are very wary about that. The story continues. When I went to Fredrick lodge I was so happy. I was the only black person on the ward. The rest were all Caucasian, white. I got on well. The food was better. Showers in your room. And there was an old nurse from Broadmoor there called Ronan and he was the ward manager. I was getting on well. I was there for 4 years. And in that 4 years I was led on a piece of string. You do this, you get that, you get discharged, you get unescorted leave you go home. At first it was ok. I didn't do any cannabis whilst I was there. I just thought this is why I was there. It was horrible hearing the things that people were talking about, about their drug abuse and what they had done. It was horrible and it was making me feel smoking. I had smoking on my mind and I was hearing about drugs all the time and just being in them places you wanted to have a little escapism, but I never did. The staff were Zimbabwean. Now I got on well with them, but boy they were hard people, hard. You know. I got excited when I got there. I found an old colleague, an old associate came to visit me. Like I said when these people came to visit me in Broadmoor I used to get myself in trouble, something would go wrong and I would have a negative vibe and I would end up in seclusion for fighting. And he visited me. And that same night I got ill and I nearly killed someone. Dr Veenan came down and said that they wanted to send me back to Broadmoor on account of the trouble. Dr Veenan said we don't want him to go back to Broadmoor, he don't need to come back. It is a slight blip, you know. Then I realised that this guy's energy is not right I don't know what he keeps on bringing home to me. But I know he is into dark sorcery you know. And I thought this guy does not want me to come out, I see that now, every time he comes around me, my mental state deteriorates and that was a close shave. I could have easily gone back to Broadmoor and I think that maybe that was his intention. So I didn't contact him again. My sister raised some issues with my solicitor's conduct, so my solicitors got vetted system in order and some couldn't come to see me. I won't go into family politics, but it was a rocky road. Anyway, from that incident I was drugged up to the eyeballs. The meds I was getting, they wake me up for it and it took about an hour to get up for it, and then I was back to bed, I went up to 22 stone. All I did was eat and sleep. I eventually got escorted leave 4 hours a week, 2 hour trips twice a week and that was what I got from there. I had a studio in my room. I managed to get a computer. A friend brought one, and they went to PACT test it and it came back that it was broken. So my mum brought one for me. I had it in my room, so I set up a studio and started recording people in there. I started making tunes and I started mixing it down. So people come and be a bit unclean in my room, I had to run them out. Then they are begging me to use it again and all that, I won't let them in. Like I say we are in hospital and they have got rules. People coming in your cells and you got rules, people coming in your room and picking their nose and farting and shit there, you know what I mean. I got the stream that we cut down recording in there. We had fun. Eventually after 4 years I got fed up of all the false promises. I rang Slam, a woman called Sarah who said they were opening a new unit in Royal Bethlem. I said look I wanna get a bed there, Sarah said she would try to get me a bed there. So I rang her every week saying come on get me out of here man, they are killing me, they are killing me. All these drugs I was on about 4 or 5 different oral meds maximum doses and maximum dose injections. I was so tired everything was an effort. But after 4 years I managed to a transfer back to the Royal Bethlem in Kent. River House, it was a new unit. When I got there I was so happy. I met Mr Mohammed and he was like "are your following me? How the hell did you know I was here". Anyway, we had a little reunion and had little talk and laugh and all that. And then I was there, they had a PD unit there they sent me there, so I have gone from mental health to personality disorder and they want to test me to see if I have a personality disorder. I am on this unit, most of the guys are white, and some of them are racist. Some of them are lifers, over half the patients. So I was there and I just got tired of the racism against the staff because the staff were mostly black. I got mad, there was a lot of shouting and arguing all the time, shouting and silly behaviour and I thought fucking hell this is noisy. I was there almost a year about 10 or 11 months. I was like fucking hell, then Duppy come down there. Duppy got discharged from Broadmoor, he was in the community. I don't know how he end up there, but he end up there and he was chatting some shit to some associates I know about me. I confronted him. He got on his hands and knees and begged me for forgiveness. I said yeah, but you see the big fancy things outta road and get badmind, try discredit man. He said ok your right I accept your apology, it is alright now and that's how it goes. That guy is here now, me and him have been solid for 10 years now, through thick and thin. My Mum bring him food. My mum visit him. To him everything was a game. It was then I realised that friendship can come and go and can be bought, the impression of all minds get stuck on to things they see and say they will say. Anything to get what they want. Because it does when it takes 10 years to come out and say these kind of things you know. It kinda piss me off, the kinda seed, but that is mankind init. So one day now, after all the tests and all that, they say that I haven't got PD so they are going to move me to

Brook. I said I don't want to go to Brook because the ward I want to go to is Chaffinch because I have heard the doctor Dr McInerny used to work in Broadmoor on Dennis ward in there and I wanted to be on his ward. So I said to them look if you put me in an alien environment I am going to start acting alien init. So they moved me to Chaffinch. I was happy. Chaffinch was alright, there was one young youth in there smoking weed and going on and on, pressing my buttons, pressing my buttons, I was saying to myself I don't want no bother here with no body but this is getting on my nerves. So one day I block up the door and called him, behave yourself, just behave yourself yeah. From there he calmed down. But he was on my case and he was driving me mad. I meet a few good guys OGs. A couple of good guys, you know, boxers the most positive one, is very positive. I was on Chaffinch from 2009 to 2011 it took ages to get my unescorted. I had escorted. For a long time I had my unescorted and it was winter and it was dark on the grounds. I had to go out and think bloody hell it is dark out here. You know I didn't feel comfortable at all. I didn't know the area or nothing, it was dark. So I used to just use my ground leave for an hour. And then eventually I got put in the flats part of the Chaffinch ward. Where you go and buy your own food for the week. They give you money, you budget, buy your own food for the week. Cook for yourself. Front room, own bedroom. And there was a phone in there. The demand for weed was very high in there and people were smoking it all the time. I tried it few times, but it didn't really agree with me so I just never really done it again. Some people were so high and they were pressurising me to get weed, weed, weed, and the place was just strong with weed that is all you could smell is weed, everyone was on it. So I find a contact and I have to buy half ounce for £40 and I brake it is down to about £300 of £20 drawers. Now I was doing that that is most money I have ever seen. From anything, even selling weed on the street, that is the most money I ever seen. You know. I was buying clothes, taking cab everywhere, having a drink. Seeing family. Putting money down. Just giving back to the family. Give them something. I was always giving them something to put into their pocket and all that. 2010 down Croydon outside Brixton's food shop, I see a beautiful empress and I thought she was smoking drugs or something, but she come up to me, start making me laugh, talk to me and I gave her my number and said just give me a call, I got to go back in. So I went back in and anyway, one day I am on the grounds outside the community centre now. I hear her voice. I said no that couldn't be her, then I see her. What you doing here? They bring me here. I was like you are joking. She said it was not good. I started joking and laugh with her reasoning and then she had to go in, I had to go in. so we used to link up, you know. Talk, I used to give her advice about medication and be careful or it will blow you up, you know. She said they were moving her, from ward to ward to ward and all that. I had to go and speak to my consultant about her and said I like her you know. I really like her. I can fall really big with her and all that. So something was arranged. I managed to have one night with her. Eventually she got discharge and asked to meet up. She would come and see me and other people she'd was doing a little thing, you know, cutting and she used to talk and doing tunes on the phone. And I would Bluetooth them to my phone and then had her number and I call her a couple of times and we talk, we talk. I took her for a drink and then I got discharge in 2011 in March, so I met her a couple of times in Croydon she said she had got a man. I was like, why is it like this. So I cool my socks. I was like up and down. I thought some girl was travelling and I was back staying at my uncles and I was travelling and then. I was just enjoying my freedom. You know going up and down, clubbing. Seeing old faces, new family members, and my mum. I was banned from Brixton so she had meet me at some niece house. I had a birthday day out, my family were there. We were at a pub having a drink and spent some time with my Mum at my family's house. I was doing well, I was focused keeping myself to myself. I was on a strict regime. I was banned from south west, and most of south east London. I was under MAPPA level 3. I was on piss test, alcohol test and my social worker was keeping me on a tight regime. Coming to see me, you can't do this you can't do that. My book was written by Tim Pritchard by this time. He was giving me £20,000 deal. I was conned out of the deal saying I am high profile and it will bring mayhem to me now I have just been released and so that fell apart and I was a bit pissed, but you know everything happens for a reason. But I was sticking to the rules and travelling on bus and Tram and I didn't really like it you know. Then Ox come to see me one time in his car and said he has got his licence and that really inspired me to go and get my licence. I asked my cousin to help me get my licence. He messed me around. So I sorted it out myself. I practiced my theory and passed first time. I rang my Empress and said I haven't seen you for a while and she said I am happy and I went to see her one time, but when I when I went to see her she was with child. I am like who's child is this now. She was my boyfriends. I'm like no or was it from that one night now. And it seemed about the right time. You know. I was constantly thinking I ain't saying nothing no. she is saying it is not mine, so I had better leave it there. Anyway, I get a phone call my Mum collapse. I am thinking it is just a little slight illness she has got. Next she is in hospital. So I go and see her, talking to her. She is talking, she is a bit poorly, but she is talking which is good. All the family that ridiculed me has come around praying, hold her and praying, praying. I questioned, saying when she needed you the most you weren't really there was you. But I never say anything. I just watched it all. Then I found out she had cancer. She got out of hospital. We had a little party for her at my niece's house. And she took sick and got took back into hospital again. No that is when I found out that she had cancer, when she went back into hospital again. Then about 2 weeks later. She went into a deep stated of consciousness, where she was lying there and not talking, eye's closed. And then we went to the hospice in Clapham. Then one day I went to go and see her and a black cat run across my path. I said that is not right, something is not right. Then my brother called me and said come. When I got to my brother's house, I said she has died init. He was crying. The mirror exploded in his house when she died. I said a black cat run across my path. I went to the hospital and my uncle was there and said she died in front of him. Family was there it was a shocking revelation to me, you know. My heart was broken. All the plans we'd made, were gone. My rock was gone. I went home that night and I remembered what I had done. Then I know my driving test was coming up, someone said cancel it. I said no way. I did it and passed, I got my licence. I got some money, got a little run around.

Jamming with family and talking to them, you know. Mum died February the 4th or 5th 2012. I can't remember what month her funeral was, but she had a good send off. Horse and cart. She got the grave spot she wanted, that's what she always said she'd wanted and she got it. It was a good night. Friends came, family came. That night I drunk, drunk, drunk brandy straight. I remember eating no food. I wasn't inside I was outside with my brother. I remember people eating and drinking. That night I went back to my uncles. He said he carried me up the stairs. I don't remember that. It was just one of those things that spiralled out of hand. My mind was playing tricks on me, I was psychotic, paranoia. My behaviour changed and I went back to the old way of how I was and thinking before I went away. Before I went away there was a girl in a shop in Croydon. I was going around her house before my mum passed away. I was helping her out, but then she done something very bad, so I had to drop her out. But before that she give me a little coke and I tried it and from then I would have a dab of coke which wasn't negative like cannabis. I got some money and bought half ounce of powder. Started dealing in my car. Driving up and down, having a smoke now and then, having a drink now and then. I didn't know, but my mind was getting worse and worse. I was thinking of violence and mixing with more people from the past. I was going places. Saying things that were very negative and silly, you know. I was in a bad way, I had misery. I was going to my brother's at 6 in the morning, 3 in the morning, 4 in the morning, waking him up out of his bed. Then I got recalled for 3 months. The home office must have felt that sorry for me and said let him have another chance. I must have lasted about 8 months before I went down Brixton, saying I was going to kill someone that made me feel very angry about the whole situation. My Mum passing and being banned from going down to see her at home. It infuriated me. I smashed up some car. I was just being reckless. I went home to my partners. She had a flat now. I was there, I was talking crazy, and she knew I was going to do something terrible. So she called the Police. But before I done that, I done something very bad, I went around her friend's house and threatened him. We spoke after that and I explained to him that my head was not in the right place, I was psychotic. He said I just changed into something different. That is the thing that people don't really understand about schizophrenia you have a few characters in you and if you are not right, nobody wants to see those characters. I apologised to him deeply and sincerely for what I had done and I broke down in tears when I done it in his house because I know what I said and was doing was totally wrong and I regret it, you know. But people think I don't really have an illness, it is just me, I can be violent, bad or aggressive or someone terrible. Anyone can be bad and aggressive. That is not me. Everyone knows me as a person who makes money, give joke and spread love. But when I was unwell I was put in a position where I felt victimised and that is how my index offence spiralled out from there and like all the talk about support, understanding and compassion, empowering someone is not there. It is all about the past, what this one said, what that one said helping me. That is not helping me at all. That is just bringing back negative thoughts in my mind and with my Mum just being gone, even family members do it. My mum just gone. They ain't helping me, they ain't empowering me, you know the past has been dark, has not been great. I have been in dark, horrible places treated bad, treated good, you know. Talk to me about something that is going to empower me. I don't want to hear about this person, that person, this, that is dead. You know. And then my Mrs called the Police and I was locked up again. I went to Landor road, by the Police and by the next day they brought me back to River House and I was on Brook ward. Needham-Bennett was my doctor. I was psychotic. No I went to Norbury the high dependency ward and I had a fight and I lost the ring my Mum gave me. Because I had a fight over the phone and they said we could not be on the same ward so they moved me to Brook. I was secluded in there. All kinds of things happened to me in there. I had never been secluded for so many days, but that was due to how ill I was. I went to Brook and met Needham-Bennett and I said Jesus, he let me know what Jesus was like. The treatment on that ward was cold, you know. There was a few good nurses and there were some bad ones. But the bad ones taught me lessons, you know. You have to respect the opportunities that you are getting. This was the second time I was back. I was treated was hard. I was locked up the whole summer. Everyone had leave, I was the only one on the ward just sitting there watching the hot days. And Needham-Bennett was just giving me injections that were making me having cramps in my body. I'd be lying in bed at night in pain and nobody came to help me. There was a young boy going through the same thing, they would rub him with pain relief cream to stop him from having the pain, but me they just left me in pain. I begged Needham-Bennett please take me off this injection and I take back the injection I was on before. Eventually he put me back on the injection I was on before and then we started to have a better understanding. He was very hard on me. The noise level in the place was so loud after being home with my family. I couldn't handle it, my head used to hurt. I met a few good guys there was a very good guy there G, he was very good hearted. Helping the youngsters, he had a son of his own. He used to take more time out for yourself and family. And they keep just coming and taking, just like in Broadmoor. A man come up to me, I give him trainers, tracksuit, food, and tobacco. I give him everything. I had loads of things, clothes I was getting in those places, I don't want to dress up and all this stuff I give away. I just wear a simple tracksuit that fit me, they are busy showering and dressing up to impress to the female nurses. I was just thinking about doing positive things and talking to my family and getting home. Just like I was when I was in Broadmoor, even in River House some of them were like that, you know. Anyway, back to Brook. So the treatment was rough, very rough. I met a dread there he seemed a good guy, but you know, everyone has got demons. There is a few good staff there. My Mrs, she showed me so much love and support. She would visit me and waited the whole year. She'd bring me food so I didn't have to eat the hospital food. Every 2/3 days groceries and things for me to cook, 5 or 6 bags of shopping was coming up to me. My clothes washed and pressed and ironed. I didn't even wash my clothes in there. I thought my Queen is a Queen, she loves me. She would park outside on the grounds and bring my daughter and have a picnic. My daughter would be playing on her scooter, running up and down, I'd watch and wave to them through the ward window. The guys would say that girl is nice, I was like behave yourself and I was just there watching the scene, my heart was touched.

 I was going through a lot therefore people who say bad things to you in the community, call the police and reported me. The nurse call me and said I should give my sister a call, as she had cursed me off and I was upset with her. I was planning on going to Jamaica and she reported me to the Home Office, saying I was selling drugs and told the Police, but I thought just let me call her. I rung her and said how are you sis and she was being a bit hostile. I just ignored her silly behaviour. I said what happened to my money and she said she spent it with her boyfriend. I said when I see your boyfriend I am going to punch him in his face, that was all I said. I was sitting in my room smoking some weed and by this time I had to do something I was in bits. I was sitting in my room crying for my Mum, there were tears just running from my eyes, so I had a little spliff, I thought that would help me. I smoked it. A staff opened my door and I said why you open my door for? He said you are on observation. Why am I on obs? What have I done wrong? I sat in my room the whole night. In the morning they said my sister said I threatened to burn down the hospital and their house. I said when have you ever seen me set fires or had any ideas of setting fires? I was on observation for about a week. The Police were coming to interview me. I found out some information about my sister, and I had to bring it to the table and the Police never came. I thought look at that my Mum has just gone, people telling lies on me. A guy that I helped in Broadmoor, brought around my family, told lies on me. I sold him my car. I made him use his driving licence, he got loads of parking tickets and I said he must pay the tickets. He gave me some of the ticket money he run up. He got recalled and told them everything. He said I threatened him, when I didn't. I was like why is everything coming on top of me. This was another guy that I showed nothing but understanding, give advice, help, empower, that is when you know friendship is a fucking funny thing. I am learning, that is not nice. I thought just look at me, I just lost my Mum and the doctor is treating me hard, some of the staff were treating me hard. The people that I thought were there for me had turned on me. I said God what is this? It is too much. It is too much to handle, why? My Mrs was coming. She kept on coming there with my daughter, bringing me food and they started saying you are treating this place like a hotel, you don't eat in here, you bring your clothes through reception and I ignored it and kept on staying focused. But it was hard. That was one of the hardest times in my life. I was weak and my rock was gone and I was being persecuted by rivals. I must have made a video on looking back on how it is living in the community. It was on you tube but I don't like the memory of that so I took it down. After a year and a month I got discharged. I said to myself never again am I going back to them places. I kept myself to myself, but I was still a bit touched I weren't fully recovered. I don't know. I was just happy to be back home with my family and Mrs and daughter. It was getting more complicated with the system and getting pressure from the hostel having early curfew restrictions. I just wanted to be home with my family. Why do I have to be in these places? These guys bother me for drugs. Silly disruptive behaviour, shout all night. Banging the floors and walls. I was like what is this? Why am I here? Why do I have to go through this? I was talking to my consultant Mr Fahy, saying come on man I want to go home. Plus

I got myself a car on hire purchase. I met this guy when I was selling this other car. My Mrs knew him as well. So I was bringing him around my house. This time I was having a pain in my side, you know a hernia, the pain was so bad I had to drive to hospital and say come and cut this out of me now. They say no you got to wait for operation. I said when is this operation gonna happen. The pain was so much I started smoking weed to help with the pain. I started smoking coke. I said to this same guy can you get me some coke. He said yes. I only find that the man was giving me grounded crack. I was wondering why my head was feeling this weird feeling. It weren't like the coke. The feeling was making me mad. I started venturing out. My Mrs was having another baby, she was pregnant. I got paranoid. I start thinking I done all these years inside and no one is giving me nothing no help. How am going to raise my family? I got 2 children to feed now and no money. So I brought some work. I started selling and dealing again. Going to clubs, buying a few drinks, breaking even, and buying a few smokes. It was a pointless adventure, pointless. All because it was unfair and I was paranoid and not in the right support from the ones that you thought were going to give it. My brother was there for me, my uncle was there for me. Talking to me a lot trying to keep me focused. Take it easy. I was grieving for my mum. I hadn't properly grieved for my Mum. The pain in me was still there, I was still hurting, I was still angry. I started linking up with friends again up and down. Going clubbing, going party, my Mrs pregnant at home. I had a hernia, I had to bring heavy shopping up 6 flights of stairs with the pain in my side. It was a lot. I had to bring my daughter to and from school. My Mrs was sick in bed due to the pregnancy, she couldn't cook or do anything much. I had to cook, clean, look after our daughter and then go out and do things at night time. Smoking, smoking and this man kept giving me powder crack that I thought was powder and I was getting more ill and ill and ill. I started doing and saying irrational things and going places acting the fool. I was just angry and hurt. I was in misery. I remember one time I was so upset about the system and everything I've been through. I drove up to Buckingham Palace and parked outside the Queen's gates and the Police said why are you doing this? I said I have come to visit the Queen. I want to talk to her about my situation. They took my name and my address and said write to her. That was how hurt I was. I don't want to talk to no Police officer, I don't want to talk to no politician, no doctor, no social worker, no psychologist, and I want to talk to the Queen who runs England to solve my problems. That is how deep and heavy my problems were. I just wanted to leave and be out of here at this time, all this. It was driving me mad, I was so upset. Anyway, I managed to decorate the whole house for my son's arrival. Whilst I was doing the work the neighbours downstairs moved out. Some people got the place. Workman started renovating the apartment, and working out of hours. My daughter trying to sleep and couldn't she'd be crying, my pregnant partner was upset. So I went there and said please can you stop working so late. They said ok, they left. All Christmas eve, all before Christmas they were banging, so they left just before Christmas day. They came back in the New Year with vengeance. I complained again. We complained to the council and Police. It was still going on, they were not responding adequately. I was getting more depressed because I was getting no sleep. I was doing and saying more silly things and going places acting peculiar. Till one day the workmen jumped me. It had been about a month since my hernia operation. I had stitches and all that still in me. There was a mesh and gauze in my stomach so I was pretty week. I got knocked out. Police came, my Mrs ran outside to defend me with her pregnant self. She went upstairs, the police came and said I have got to go to hospital. I said what for? This time I was totally oblivious to what had happened, I couldn't remember. Police took me to hospital and give me some x-rays and all that. I was like what is going on, I don't remember nothing. I was totally confused. Police took me back home. Took a picture of my face and emailed my doctor. I got in the bath. I didn't get a chance to get out the bath the front door knock. It's the police, 8 of them this time, they said I am under arrest for assault. I thought what the hell are you on about? They took me to the station. I was in there from Friday to Monday. My Mrs is about to have my baby. She is ringing me on the phone at the station. Saying don't worry, don't worry, don't worry. I said has the baby come. She said no he will wait for you. I'm like, what is going on. I am confused. My heart is hurting me. I got pain in heart. My heart is just pounding. The Police took me to the hospital. I thought I was going to have a heart attack. They are talking to me. Saying just take it easy. The Monday I went to court, I just prayed. I got bailed. I thought wow. The bail condition was I had to leave my Mrs Address by nightfall. I can't be there certain times during the day either. She came to pick me up. Then bam…. my son came 28th January. I was there, I cut the umbilical cord and took him up and hug him and gave him a kiss. I said you know that is a miracle I just seen there. My Mrs had ectopic pregnancies before my son came and she thought she would never be able to have another child. But I prayed about it and he came out healthy and strong at almost 9lbs. and that is when I said I am going to change my life. This is a blessing. A new start and I told her this and I sat with her all night and then I went home. My daughter was with my niece. They keep my Mrs in the hospital few days. But where my daughter was with my niece I didn't like the look of her brother. So I got my daughter and went to my Mrs and said you are coming home. After 2 days she came home. I had to leave them, I had to leave early I had to be in and out at a certain time. The workmen were still banging down the place. I am saying to myself. What the hell is this? A new born baby, daughter crying, Mrs needs to relax and they are banging down the place. I am trying to find out who these workmen are. I was asking people, but no one knew nothing. They are saying do you want us to come down there and sort it out. I didn't want that. The Police and Mental health service had me on all these restrictions, so I couldn't do anything. I was getting sicker and sicker after the incident of hitting my head. My head was totally gone, you know. I used to go to my hostel and there were workmen there banging. How come everyone is banging everywhere? I can't get no peace in this distressed state of mind. So I started to lose it. This particular night I was on one in the house, talking to myself and basically going into deep psychosis. My partner called the Police and asked them to escort me to the hostel as I'm unwell. They wanted to know if I hit her, she said no, I never hit her. So they escorted me outside the building and left. I had my key so I went back upstairs and slept in the front room. In the morning, when I said I was going to take my daughter shopping, my Mrs said no. Not in that state of mind. But I persisted and said I want to take my daughter shopping and spend some time with her. My poor Mrs said no, not in that state of mind. She called my social worker, at a time when I wasn't meant to be there. He said is he there? She said yeah. We argued, I left, got in my car. All of a sudden I was surrounded. Police came around, 20 of them, 6 cars, 1 van, 1 ambulance, and they took me out the car and off to the Police station. From there I got recalled back to River House. It was the worst mistake I ever made. I was sent to Kneesworth House in Cambridgeshire. Miles and miles away from my partner and kids for around 11 months, I was in there. It was the most maddest place I have ever been. Pure mad people, totally off their heads. Fighting, giving each other stitches. My hernia wound is hurting me where I had the operation. My heart is hurting me. I was in pain and I can't defend myself and these guys are fighting like cat and dog. I'm like what is this man? You know. I am praying, I'm praying. I'm reading my bible. I am reading the New Testament now. I started picking up things about how to deal with the situation in there, don't argue with fools. You can't argue with a fool. My Mrs rang me about 4 or 6 times a day. Just hearing her voice and talking to her was soothing. I was just closing my eyes, and visualising myself, away from that place, being back home with my family. The guys in there started getting jealous and hounding me on the phone, blocking it and doing all kinds of perplexing things to provoke me. I was thinking this is annoying. The staff were great, really supportive and helped me a lot. The doctor was hard. She was the one who wouldn't talked to me. It took a lot of persuading to get her to talk to me, she started to help. I had a good young social worker, but my team were back home were just not responding. I was dumped there. My heart felt like I was having a heart attack. I was driven and escorted in handcuffs through the general hospital on 3 separate occasions. People just looking at me, thinking I must have done a crime. What is happening to me? The things I was saying to people in the community. How I was behaving. This is my karma, I have got to accept it. I was looking rough, my face not shaved, hair uncombed, dry and picky. In the same tracksuit two days and change into another tracksuit. That was all I was wearing. The place was dirty and it was the most vile smelling place you could imagine. It stunk of foot, sweat, B.O. You know. There was another young guy in there with something to prove decided to try victimise me. Throwing his weight around, pushing me when I was in the dinner queue, bouncing whilst passing me, just on my case. They moved him opposite me. I'm like how am I going to stop this. So I ran up in his room and tied him up, me with my sick self. Then the little fucker grassed me up. I thought I can't have this. What am I meant to do in a situation like this? The staff were supportive. They reassured me saying don't worry, don't worry. Soon after, I had a Tribunal and lost it. I don't know what they said about the situation and everything. They had no understanding. I said yep this is definitely my karma. Definitely. My Mrs kept on phoning. She phoned so much I didn't want to talk to her. I just wanted out of there. The smoking was only allowed because it was a private hospital and they had parts you could smoke. You can't smoke after 8 o'clock at night. But I had a light, so I would smoke in my room, but it was getting on top of me, so I gave it away. They searched me and couldn't find it, by then I had given it away. The place was rough. Man was just getting punched up daily. Getting cut, smashed in the face. I was like what kind of place is this man. It was constant chaos, no order. Blood was flowing 24/7. This one going hospital, that one going hospital. I was like no man, I have got to get out of this war zone.

Anyway November 2015 I made it back to River House on Chaffinch ward. The guy who grassed me up about the car business and said I threatened him was on the same unit. The ward staff made us both sign a peace treaty stating that we are not going to argue or fight. I just signed it and had no intention of troubling him. He kept on telling me his problems, but I had my own problems. I couldn't see my kids. I couldn't see my Mrs. I couldn't be that rock for no man in here again. My Mrs already warned me not to get involved too much with these guys in here again, not after what has happened previously. The guy got jealous due to my conscious lack of time for him and started acting silly. Spreading malicious lies. Trying to make snide comments saying to people he was up to no good with my Mrs. I was his pain. But I wasn't interested. I stayed in my room, I had to stay in my room. I'd come out to get food, meds etc. I smoked in my room and talked to my Mrs on my phone. By this time you could have a simple mobile, that was the best thing ever, you know. I kept myself to myself as I knew now I had something special at home to stay focused and motivated for. Like 99% of these man in here had 0 to get out for

I want to talk about one time when I was psychotic in Broadmoor. I had a psychotic episode for about a week. The episode was recorded. It stated that in 1994 I said that I died and came back as a dog and the politicians and the Queen were all my new friends. I was barking like a dog. I put on a suit and said I was going to see Tony Blair. I was secluded and I was given some medication and when I came back round it came in like a dream. It just seemed so real, when I was in that state of mind. I want to talk about when I was in River House, all the therapeutic interventions I had. I done over 3 drug and alcohol groups and some lasted for over 20 weeks. Even when I was discharged I was going back to do them. I done relationship group. I done education and got certificates in River House. I made music and a YouTube video at River House. I done relapse prevention, psychotherapy, one to one, I done so much different therapy groups.

Let me get back to when I got recalled for the third time. I was in Kneewsworth House and I said it was a terrible place, a mad place with the illest people I have ever seen. I had phone in my cell and my Mrs would call me and I would talk to her also my brother, my uncle. The ward manager from Chaffinch called Jane came to see me, when she saw me she was shocked. I was the worst I have ever been in hospital. I looked very rough. She said she was trying to get me on Chaffinch pre discharge ward. It took a little while before I got leave and it took a longer time to get unescorted. There were a few problems. Saying how I had to do certain things and all that. When I got back some of the patients were there that I knew they had also been recalled. Some of them were smoking weed again, some were smoking crack, some were smoking spice and then they were trying to entice me into getting it and smoking it. But I spent most of my time by myself in my room and there was no associate with no one. I wanted to learn about myself and what made me tick. And what was my downfalls and all my life's experiences. I was evaluating them. I had to be alone. So I had a mobile phone in my cell and my Mrs would call me and I would talk to her. Most of the time it was when I got news from the doctor or social services involvement and I can't see my children for now. And they would knock and say I have got a gift for you. I would say, what's the gift, and I see big lump of crack. I go that is no gift for me, go away from my door with that, a Rasta bringing me that worst of all. I thought no man, this is some heartless moves, they see I am down and pressuring me taking crack ain't going to solve my problems. When I was a young person with no responsibilities and was silly that might have been an escape route for me, but not at that stage, I wanted to go home to my family. I had a good psychotherapist called Ken who I worked with for a discharge programmes and care plans. He was very sympathetic and understanding that even though I was under a great deal of pressure. I finally got my unescorted and I spent most of my time going home and spending time with my daughter and son and my fiancée. I would go home and go back to the unit, back and forth. I was able to show my late mum and my brother that we had done it. Now I wanted to christen my kids, so I organised that and I organised the christening of my great nephew. Some dispute came up and I went to their christening, but they never came to mine. That was kinda bad after I organise it for them, but such is life. We were going to have them together, but it was getting silly so we split them up and that is how it went. Christened my children and I met my partners father and family for the first time and my brother and family were there. It was a good day. I had to go back to hospital I had a leave till about 2 in the morning and I went back about 1.45. My leave was getting extended, I was getting 12 hours leave. The 12 hours were going fast. I had a Tribunal, where Dr Tim McInerny was backing me, but on the process of going into the Tribunal I heard the layman or the doctor saying I am not going to let this man go and I should cancel the Tribunal when I went in. But I thought no let me just try my luck. I went in and I said hello to all apart from the layman or doctor who wasn't having it. He said I am a bad Dad, he said I have done all these therapies. Victim awareness, parenting therapy, index therapy, psychotherapy, he had a long list. Dr McInerny tried to defend me, but the man start to gun Tim McInerny down for his opinion that I should be discharged and I lost the Tribunal. And I thought I was getting out, because with the doctor backing you, you usually do. Both were equal and he wasn't having it. I was heartbroken, but I picked myself back up and continued pushing on. I started doing the therapies and that is when I started doing this course restorative justice, learning about your victims and the ripple effect that your crimes have and maybe one day you can meet your victims and apologise for the crimes you have done. It is a very good course and it is a level 1 to 3 and with restorative justice, I have a certificate saying I have a level 3 ranking. I done it. I learnt a lot. I wrote a letter to all of my victims saying sorry for what I done and saying I wasn't in a good frame of mind when I done the crimes and I am sorry for what I done and I was immature and irresponsible and wrong and I hope they can accept my apology and if one day they would like to meet me, to talk and find out more why these crimes occurred or what led to them I would be willing to meet them. I met with Dr Gerrard at the course. I thought he was just an O.T., he was a lead psychologist. He invited me to a seminar with Dr Fahy and Dr McInerny to where they talk about my index offence and how they occurred and what my mental state was like. I went to a seminar in Royal Institute of Psychiatry, it was a very uplifting experience. I have been invited to a few talks about mental health and the ways to treat people. And the best way to approach people who are unwell.

My Tribunal was coming up in November 2016. I said to myself. I have gotta win this one. This one is coming to be my third Tribunal in the coming up for 2 years I have been away, for a crime I hadn't done. For being beaten up charged, but I just say it is my karma and I have got to deal with it, you know. Before the Tribunal came up I wrote to the Home Office explaining my case and saying that I have learnt from my experiences. I know I have acted inappropriate in the community but I don't believe I deserve this treatment. On November 30th I received a letter saying they were going to release me and they discharged me. I have been out ever since. I was discharged to a hostel. The hostel was nice. The staff were nice, but there was some ill patients giving me problems and one was above me. So every night I came home from my family, he would make noise all night pacing, stamping so I couldn't sleep. I complained to the hostel manager, my doctor, my social worker. The guy wouldn't stop. It was getting on my nerves. I thought look at this from one fire to another. Eventually I got home to my family.

I done everything that was asked of me. You know I am not meeting with criminal associates. I am keeping myself to myself. So I am on the right track. I need a chance. So after months of being in the hostel I moved to my family's home. Then I got some more good news I was taken off MAPPA. I thought wow this is great. So this is coming up to my second year of being out. In this process I have been working in Recovery College. Working as a peer trainer, going back into River House teaching and training patients and staff. I am on the involvement register with SLAM. I've been going back doing seminars and speeches. Dr Gerard and Fin who worked on the restorative justice have contacted me and asked me to help then write a programme called Kintsugi a Japanese methodology, like a pot or bowl that is broken, you repair it with 24 carat gold to make it stronger than and better than what it was before. So then the hope that the whole philosophy of life you have things that can make you break or come down, like people in hospital who have a mental illness so they want to have my methods and ways of how to survive in my situations and problems and bring it back to the forum and teach the people, empower them, to enable them, to give them the knowledge to help them get over their mental illness and I thought, I feel honoured and privileged to be in the position like that. I am doing an NVQ level 3 in support and guidance. I am just looking forward to the future and this is me here recording my notes for the next part of my book to be added and one day I hope for my book to be released. I have had 3 bad record deals and out of all the record deals I have earnt £400. Your music is not current music that everyone appeals to. You are not modern day stuff, but this is a lot of philosophy, good stuff and reasoning and powerful songs. Some negative ones, not talking about them, just like my past experience of how I felt and how I have seen things, but there are some positive songs that lift or teach. I just want hope that one day a record label will give me a chance to get my music aired and played and let people hear my story. I have been home with my home with my family now for almost a year and a bit now. Settling in with the kids and establishing a routine. Getting to know my Mrs better and work together as a team. She is the most blessed woman I have ever met. She has done so much for me. And then wishing my spirit soul and mine to make me the person I am today, with my experience and myself acknowledge. And we debate and reason and we talk and we both come from colourful and dark pasts. But we have learnt from them. We just want to do great things together. To raise our children the best and right manner and give them the best that they deserve as our children are Prince and Princess, our angels. They really are now my pushing point in life. Keep me grounded and focused.

Being back in the community I've found most of the people who know you have a mental health issue and associate with them, are prejudice/judgemental. Accompanied with all the pressures you have got to deal with and still maintain, run your family, just daily living. It shouldn't be like this, you know. I watch everyone soaking it up like they want you to react to the bullshit like you're crazy and make a fool of yourself when they put you through these frustrating unnecessary situations. But that is just their stupidity and ignorance rather than trying to empathise and understand someone. This is annoying and very frustrating. As Jesus said "let he who is without sin cast the first stone". I think everyone should try and practise that. For real!!

Well it is coming to the end of my book. My life has been like a rollercoaster with many ups and downs, thankfully I have learned and become a stronger and wiser person. I just want to do good, give back and I am extremely grateful for the opportunity I have to give something back, to those who are in hospital and try reach out to them, because mental health has a very big stigma that has to be broken, anybody can get ill, anyone can have ill health. Sickness is indiscriminate. I am sure many have got someone in their family or friends that suffer with poor mental health, don't judge or ridicule them. Try and help. Talk with them and seek professional advice from a GP or hospital A&E if necessary

Jamaican Heritage.

This is my Jamaican heritage that I learnt from my Uncle James who is like a father figure to me. Who taught me all my Jamaican history, from my grandmother to my great grandmother to my great grandfather and my aunties and uncles and my family in Jamaica. My Uncle James is 96 this year and is still alive, and going strong, cooking and cleaning for himself. His like a father figure I had because I never knew my father, who left just after my birth. Uncle told me that George William Gordon whose mother was a slave, self-educated, owned land in St Thomas. He owned sugar cane plantations and became a Prime Minister Hero for his parish in Jamaica. He was a cousin of mine. My other cousin was Paul Bogle who run the revolutionary act in St Thomas and helped Jamaica get independence. My great grandfather was Tartar Logan he was a carpenter, a Deacon, a butcher and he made all the coffins for the people who died in the parish. Then my grandmother aunt May, my mother's mum and my grandfather had 3 girls and 2 boy. My great grandmother was a maroon and had 10 girls and 4 boys with my great granddad, the family was a big family in St Thomas. They had a lot of say in St Thomas there were 3 main families that run St Thomas and mine was one of them. My family was made up of teachers, soldiers. Teachers were the great career that most of my family took. I had 2 cousins who fought in World War 2 and I heard that they were well off in Jamaica and they were the ones who got most of land after the slaves were freed and the Europeans had left the land, they took control of the land. My uncles, some of them were well established. My aunties were well established, some owned shops. My grandmother used to set up the market. I never knew this family history and I felt honoured to have such a strong heritage of Jamaican history.

My Uncle James told me all of this and when I was down and frustrated, I would listen to his methods and teaching to cope and get through all the hard times I was going through. He would talk to me all the time I had been away, he had been a great rock to me and I love him dearly. I try my best to support him. It is getting harder now I am trying to support my family and be rock to him that I have been and continue to be a rock for him. I got a large family in England, a lot of cousins, uncles and aunties. I don't really see much of them. There is only a few that I am in contact with and we talk regular, but the family network is very vast. I had a cousin who was kill outside Brixton Police Station in about 2012 he was stabbed in the heart. I met that cousin at my mother's deathbed which was a great loss to me and pain, as it brought up my mother's death and I saw the sense of what actions I take, what actions I do have impacts on families, you know. I was very torn up about it and someone offered me a gun to kill the boy's father and I said to myself you know what. Do you think that man hasn't learnt that lesson and hasn't changed and I just walked away from the situation and left it to the courts of justice to whatever will be the fate, you know.

I know my childhood experiences and growing up and becoming a man. I have learnt, I have had a very hard rocky road. I have learnt that I never had a chance to be a boy. I had to be a man fast. I was supporting my family. My mother is worked and she done her own thing, she didn't want money from me like the rest of my family. I gave them a lot of money, supported their children, you know, when I was doing my negative road stuff. I supported a lot of people in the community. I had people phoning me for food, rent, electric, gas. I see people on the street and I give them money to buy trainers. The environment was very poor. It was a very hard time. I want people to remember these things I have done for them. I am not saying I want anything back for it, because I didn't give to receive. I just know it was hard times everyone was going through and I was getting money like a Robin Hood kind of character doing wrong, but I tried to do good. I think that made some despise my character. I had principles, morals that my mother taught me. I tried to do them and live by them even though I was doing wrong and I became a victim of the streets.

I have done 20 years off of incarceration. I have had about 4 years off and on in the community in about 20 years. And I am now trying to rebuild my life. I have 2 children and a fiancée. I don't get much support from most of my family, you know. But the ones who do support me I thank you and love you dearly for that. And I wish there was more support, as I was supportive to most of my family, but that is how things are. But it hurts to know that what you do for others they won't do for you. But you have to live and learn and it makes you stronger and wiser. I wish all the people I have met in my life well. Wish them the best. I have no animosity or hate towards no one. No negative feeling, no negative thoughts, you know. I have learnt from my experiences and I am a better, reformed character.

Street life is not all it is made out to be kids or youngster, all those who are getting indoctrinated into crime. It is a hell of a rollercoaster and some don't make it out alive, some go to jail for life or some become a victim of drugs and never be able to get off them. Some will be a victim of violence, being in the system and drugs. Now I have a few damaged feathers, but I am still trying to fly straight. Still showing love by going back into hospital and helping those less unfortunate than me.

My music artist name Hoggie Dogg, I hope to get the right publicity and air play as there is a lot of positive messages in there. I don't want to talk about the negative stuff, because I came from a negative background and everyone talking about a scene I have been involved in or heard or experienced. I just want to say God is good in all the rest of this. God is good. One day I wish to go to Jamaica and pay respects to my grandparent's tomb and I've never been in an aeroplane and one day I wish to go on holiday. So from me to you I hope you enjoyed reading my story. Wayne Hutchinson or ……….. You will never know and if you do, don't think it is glamourizing gangsterism. Peace.

Family Issues

So this is just me and my nephew talking about family issues that we want added to the manuscript. So Dee begin.

Dee: well, I picked this up from October 1994, so just before October 1994 that was my 12th birthday. I remember going around to my grandma's house. I remember you coming downstairs, having just woken up at whatever time it was about half four and he was just acting a bit strangely he said happy birthday and how are you bruv and I said I was fine and you kept saying to me are you alright and I kept saying I was fine. And then you know, about 2 minutes later you were like are you alright and I was yeah I'm fine and this went on for about half an hour so. And then there was a things. A very strange look on his face and his eyes and stuff and even at 12 I knew that something wasn't right. I didn't know what it was, but I knew something wasn't right and then as the rest of the year went on the change became more and more evident. And then leading up to the index offence and then the aftermath. From then it was a while before I saw the old you again. I started to see flashes of it. But it took a while before we saw the real him back. Yeah so as a result he has had some interesting experiences and long train journeys with some very interesting characters. And seeing and being a part of a very long train journey that's coming to a new start. No let's say a new chapter. Coming to a new side and err. I think that for a lot of courage and perseverance, you have come through the other side and I think that Wayne has the opportunity to do the things he always wanted and suppose to do. And that is be a more positive influence on those around him, like he was for me when I was younger. I think that is about it.

Wayne: thank you Dee. So that explains the psychosis. Psychosis is a phenomenal thing, you said when I was going through it. I was looking strange and there was a journey before I was back to myself. So you know mental illness is a journey.

Dee: it certainly is and you know on that journey you have very many stops sometimes. You know you go back, you go a few steps forward and as a result of those few steps forward you just think yeah I have beat this, I am there. And then it just pulls you back in.

Wayne: yeah you go back, definitely.

Dee: you've had many conversations on the phone where you had said you just want be out of this place. I want to do this, I want to do that. And it is like nope, you need to take the time. I know you have been there a long time and don't want to be there but you have got to get the process through. You know, I have said to you before, it is something I believe the place you found yourself, is the place you need to be at that point, I was looking at the life you were living and the people who were around you at the time, many of them aren't here anymore or are still away for the rest of their lives or there is that we are lucky enough to avoid those things are still basically the people that they were 25 years ago. They are not doing anything of any of note or anything with their lives. Whereas you have been, as a result of those experiences you can now talk to people or young people about those experiences and about how to talk to them about the point of those experiences and speak to them on a different level. And then they know that you are not just someone who has a theory of what it is like to go through those experiences, you have actually experience. You said you have been through the fire and you know you didn't say you didn't get burnt because you were burnt, but those wounds are healing now and you are back to being that positive influence you have always appeared to be and I think you had to go through that experience in order to come out the other side, have that perspective of things.

Wayne: the insight.

Dee: Yeah.

Wayne: definitely. One thing we will go through, we will tell them kids, if you play with fire you will be burned.

Dee: for sure.

Wayne: and when we are kids we don't listen and sometimes you have to go through the flames to be purified or learn or understand wrong from right. That what we was taught from day one. So it is a lesson for you youngsters, you must listen to your parents for they are giving you good advice. And if they are giving you bad advice, you should seek good advice.

Dee: for sure.

Wayne: not everyone is giving good advice, but you hear good advice eat it, swallow it up and let it enrich your brain. The way society is nowadays it is very confusing, internet, media, what you can see. You know. It's like the old way is dying. It is the last of dying breed out here. The new generation is just fast and confusion. Hype and craziness. You need to get back to the logistics of things. And be happy with everyday life, basic necessity. Be happy in your surrounding and comfort zone. Don't venture out too far, because there are wolfs in the woods.

We are going to leave it there. That is my nephew Dee, no more names. I want to big up Dee.

Dee: just remember my percentage when the book sells hahaha.

Wedding date 10 August 2019

Wedding Speech

I had the greatest teacher my Late Great Mother Judith , but I had a another teacher the streets

Which took to me a dark place, while there I fasted and pray to leave

I went to my meeting

I was told to stay in my dark place

I remember asking God All I want is a Queen to love me for me

Before Stepping Back in the Light I found my Queen

A year later my Mother was called to Heaven

I was confused but I had my Love who fought with everything with my 2 Angels to get her King back to safety

Only thing which was on our side was Love and God

I know there are forces which tried to come between us but let me tell you all this Real Love and God plan

So respect what God has in store for us

To my Queen Today we make it Official

Your a great rock, Mother, Lady of my dreams

without you I would not be here today

Love, Respect And Honour My Queen For Life

Thanks to the Bridesmaids & Groomsmen

My 2 brothers my best men

Mother & Father in-law

Family's and Friends

My 1 only Sister

Thanks You For Coming To Witness's Our Great Day

Of 2 Becoming 1

God Bless

I would like to thank my wife for making this book possible.